An Interesting Life Devoted to God
(For the Most Part)

By:

— William S. Bunte

Order this book online at www.trafford.com
or email orders@trafford.com

Most Trafford titles are also available at major online book retailers.

Print information available on the last page.

ISBN: 978-1-4120-9482-5 (sc)

Trafford rev.   09/23/2016

 www.trafford.com

North America & international
toll-free: 1 888 232 4444 (USA & Canada)
fax: 812 355 4082

Acknowledgements

Many, many thanks to my wife, Jean, and to my good friend, Dick Birmingham, for great suggestions and advice, and for the many hours they spent in recommended corrections. (The "spell-check" on my computer was not working, which didn't help).

Introduction

I never once thought about writing a book about my life, and if I had I am sure that I would not have done so. However, when God told me to write such a book, he even told me the title of the book; then I had to take this request more seriously.* This is hard to believe. However, during my life I have heard God tell me to do certain things, and when I did them, miracles happened! I will tell you about them in this book.

One question has been bothering me as I write this book. Why did God pick me to write a book? I know many men who are much holier than I am.... But God must know what he is doing! Even if just one person gets closer to God after reading this book, it will be worthwhile!

This book is an autobiography, and not a novel, so what I have written is true to the best of my memory. Each day, before I would start writing, I would pray to the Holy Spirit to guide me in what to say, and to remember the important times of my life. It was amazing how certain items came to me, when I haven't thought about them for many, many years.

I am also sure the Holy Spirit had something to do with my keeping all the articles, photos, etc. that you will see. Many times I was ready to "clean out" these and other items that were in my files that I didn't think I would ever look at again, but for some reason I never did get around to it. Now I know why!

I write the stories in this book, not for what I have done, but what God has done through me...

During World War 11, no one on our ship (USS Mona Island) was allowed to have a camera except the ship's photographer. While we were overseas, I got to know him very well. When the war was over, he gave me copies of many of the pictures he took. He also knew the photographer who took the famous photo of the Japan surrender on the USS Missouri, and he gave me a copy of that also.

---

* (I actually heard His voice)

In some sections of this book, I have added quite a bit of detail for those who might be interested in it, however, I am sure that there will be some who will not have that same interest. Examples might be the detailed agendas of some of the trips and pilgrimages that I took, and my various experiences while working for certain companies, such as Egan Machinery.

I found a book at the library that compared the value of money from 1920 (and any year since then), and what that price would be today. You will find that I used this several times in this book.

William S. Bunte

Chapter 1

Early Life

I was born May 2, 1923 in Lexington, Ky on my mother's race horse farm, Elsmead. I found out later that one of the horses raised there, won the Kentucky Derby.

My mother was Helen Skain (Bunte). She went to high school at a Convent where she became a Catholic, and then graduated from the University of Kentucky. She was of Irish descent. I was always interested in my ancestors, and while my grandparents were still alive, I was able to obtain a lot of information on the family background. I found out that through my mother, I was related to an Irish saint - Oliver Plunket.

My father was Chester Bernard Bunte. His father was German and his mother was English. He went to the University of Colorado, but left before he graduated to join the army, and served in the First World War. He was injured during one of the battles. After the war was over, he took his first airplane ride with a friend, who was a pilot during the war. They were flying over Paris when the engine quit. They crash landed in someone's back yard! Fortunately, they were not seriously hurt; however, my father never wanted to fly again. He did fly occasionally but only when he had to - even with the modern airplanes. Fortunately I didn't inherit that fear. I loved to fly, and would ride in a plane whenever I had a chance.

After my birth, we only stayed a few weeks in Kentucky. We then moved to Okmulgee, Oklahoma where we lived for three years. My father got into the oil business, so we moved to Tulsa, Oklahoma which was close to the wells that were being drilled at the time. He started out as a laborer and worked his way up to a promoter where he would raise money by leasing the land owner's land to oil companies. The money that was raised would be used to pay for drilling the well as well as paying the land owner for the leases on his land. My father would receive any money that was left over after these obligations were paid. If not enough money was received, then my father would have to pay the difference. However, when the well hit oil, then, if he had any leases left, he could make a large profit. He did "hit" a large oil well in East Texas. Instead of saving most of this profit, he purchased a larger house in Tulsa, and invested the rest in new wells, which were "dry holes". We then moved to a smaller house in San Antonio, Texas. This is the way we lived. In fact, my father's "calling card" showed: a small house, a large house, a small house, etc. We lived in Tulsa for three years. We had a large garden at our house in Tulsa. One time my grandfather came to visit us. He said we raised the largest peanuts he had ever seen. He showed us where he thought they were buried. He had buried them there earlier in the day.

My father (on right) during first World War.

My father and I

My father in garden.

My father & I at oil well.

My second birthday party.

C. B. BUNTE, ESPERSON BLDG., HOUSTON, TEX.
"First he drills a dry hole, then a gusher, then a dry hole,
then a gusher, etc., etc."

We dug them up and each peanut was six inches in diameter and 12 inches long! When we opened the "peanuts" we found a different toy in each one! The other thing I remember about Tulsa was the terrible thunder and lightning storms. One day during one of these storms, I was looking out the window, and saw lightning hit a telephone pole which was at the top of a hill. A four to five foot diameter ball of fire fell to the ground, and rolled all the way to the bottom of the hill!

In San Antonio, I went to a Catholic grade school, St. Anthony's. My fourth grade nun was a great teacher, and for some reason she took a special interest in me. She gave me various religious articles, including a copy of a painting of the Little Flower which I still have. One day she asked me to stay after school. She asked if I had ever thought of going to daily Mass. I said that I went to Sunday Mass with my mother, but my father didn't go to church at all. The nun suggested that I try daily Mass for one week, and then make a decision. I didn't say "yes" or "no", but evidently the Holy Spirit convinced me to try it. Since then, I have been a daily communicant whenever it was possible. There have been times when I have been traveling on business, was sick, during combat when I was in the Navy during the 2nd World War, etc. when I was unable to go to Communion. I was fortunate that there was a Catholic Chaplain on our ship who conducted daily Mass whenever possible. Another priest told me about a "Spiritual Communion" where you ask God to come into your heart, and you pray just as you would in regular Communion. I use this whenever I am not able to go to Mass. With God's help and encouragement, I have been a daily communicant since that decision in fourth grade.

I loved my father very much, but he didn't think too much of my going to Mass every day. He was always up very early every morning planning his business day. I would have to go past him

5

to get my bike. Although he didn't say I couldn't go to Mass, I decided to go out my second story bedroom window, climb down a tree to the ground, and ride my bike the three miles to church. Then I would ride back home, climb back up the tree, and come downstairs to breakfast!

My father took home-movies of the family since I was born, and I was the oldest. He thought so much of these movies that when we moved, he hired an armored truck just to move them!

I had two sisters, Nanette and Helen, and two brothers, Jack and Pat. I am blessed, for they are all still living.

My mother on farm before marriage.

My mother and I.

Farm where I was born.

In San Antonio, Texas, I had a good friend, David, who lived in the house across the street. We dug a large hole in the vacant lot near us and covered the top with old boards and called it our "Club House". We had to slide down an opening to get inside. The only problem was that snakes could also get inside. After we saw a rattlesnake inside our Club House several weeks later, we covered the hole back up!

We had a German Shepard dog named "King". He was a great dog for us children. He would let my younger brothers and sisters ride him just like a horse. One day he was in the vacant lot next to our house, and he was bitten by a rattlesnake. My father took him to a veterinarian across town about 15 miles away, left the dog with the vet, and came back home. A short time later, the vet called to say that King got out of his pen, and they had not been able to find him. Two weeks later, King found his way back to our house, and died by the front door! To us kids, it was like one of us had died...

One day my friend David and I decided to visit a new boy in our neighborhood, Jack. We got in a mild disagreement with Jack and decided to leave. After we got back on the street, we heard a gunshot. We looked back, and Jack was on a second story porch, shooting at us with a rifle! I told my father about it, and he reported it to the police. Evidently Jack had other such problems on this record, so he was sent to some type of reform school for minors.

While I was living in San Antonio, I went to a "Cowboy Camp" about 50 miles north of San Antonio. I learned how to ride Western Style and Bareback (no saddle). We also went on horseback trips for two or three days. At night, we slept out under the stars. The guides would put a thick rope around the sleeping area to keep the snakes away from us. This seemed to work, for we saw a lot of snakes in the area, but, thank God, none came where we were sleeping.

When I was in 5th grade I delivered magazines to local households in San Antonio with my bicycle. One of the magazines was the "Liberty." I recently received a certificate showing that I was "Honorably Discharged" from the "Army of Liberty Boys!"

OLIVER
PLUNKETT

DESMOND FORRISTAL

OLIVER PLUNKETT: *MARTYR*

Edward M. Curley

John McKee tells us, "The Holy Father has lamented repeatedly that Christians today are being tempted to think horizontally––devoting themselves to secular causes––instead of vertically, to God." He continues: "Time for them to look Oliver Plunkett in the face!"

One of the more recent saints, Oliver was canonized October 12, 1975. A shepherd whom we would be proud to follow, he had but one concern and that was the saving of souls. With eyes on this goal, he forged ahead, completely disregarding his own safety. While aware of peripheral activities, he did not permit them to sidetrack him from the main issue.

As is the case with the majority of saints, Oliver ripened slowly under the guidance of the Holy Spirit. Going to Rome in 1647 at the age of eighteen to study for the priesthood, he was to remain there almost twenty-five years. After ordination he submitted his petition to stay in Rome, primarily because the climate in Ireland was extremely hostile to the Catholic Faith. He was not yet ready to offer his life in martyrdom. His wish was granted. He could bend with the wind or remain steadfast. Oliver, himself, said, "Don't give way to the wicked but tackle them more boldly."

Standing steadfast would, of course, mean drawing on the infinite grace available through the prayers and sacrifices of his life. This he did.

Here's a shepherd who stayed clear of politics, ministered to his flock under the most trying conditions of anti-Catholicism, suffered from bone-chilling cold and lack of food, administered a "See" with ten of its eleven dioceses vacant and the one that was filled held by a sick, aged bishop, plagued with apostate priests and renegade laity and, in general, with little going for him. Despite these tremendous handicaps, he established several schools, confirmed some 50,000 Catholics in the first four years and worked amicably with Protestant officials. He spent the following twelve years teaching theology at the College of Propaganda in Rome.

In expressing concerns for a friend's vulnerability in ministering to victims of the plague, he received this in reply, "Why do you fear, oh you of little faith? . . . Place your trust in God and He will do everything." This thunderbolt of truth stayed with our Saint. Some years later when the Archbishop of Armagh in Ireland died, Oliver volunteered and was appointed by the Vatican even though he had not been nominated. We can imagine Pope Clement smiling as he said, "Why waste time in discussing the dubious merits of others, whilst we have here in Rome a native of that island whose merits are known to us all?"

Consecrated in Belgium, Oliver first went to England and was received hospitably by the catholic queen. Donning a disguise to elude the priest-chasers, he arrived in Ireland surviving for some fifteen months often without shelter, occasional straw for bedding and with very poor food. He was well aware that every bishop has two choices; he extolled preaching as a way of educating the ill-informed, celebrated Mass even "if the altar was sometimes as unbaroque as a mossy boulder," and all this whilst tightening the controls upon his diocese.

Finally, the anti-Catholic bigotry was fanned in a conflagration through the calumnies and lies of those who were either hostile to his efforts or the apostates who wished him dead. Through lies, perjuries, and refusals to let him testify in his own behalf or call witnesses, he was summarily sentenced to death, hung, bowels ripped out and decapitated. Although later vindicated of all charges, his "trial" and death stand both as a rebuke to prejudice and a monument of orthodoxy and loyalty to the Pope. The example of his life and death most certainly leaves a message for all those who seek guidance in times of hostility and dissension.

In an address to the international Union of Mothers General, Pope John Paul II said:

"If your consecration to God is such a deep reality, it is not unimportant to bear permanently its exterior sign which a simple and suitable religious habit constitutes: it means to remind yourselves constantly of your commitment which contrasts strongly to the spirit of the world; it is a silent but eloquent testimony; it is a sign that our secularized world needs to find its way, as many Christians, moreover, desire. I ask you to turn this over carefully in your minds."

BUNTE FAMILY TREE
(Mother's Side)

1500

Lord Plukett   Great Grandfather of
1   James Monroe (5th Pres).
1   1
1   Miss Monroe (Daughter of Pres)
1   1
Bayon John Plunkett   Sir Luke Dillon
1   1
1   1

1600

1   1
1   Thomoniasina Dellon
1   1

1   1   1   1   1   1
1   1   1   1   1   1
1   Oliver Plunkett   1   Ann Plunkett   1   Mary Plunkett
1   (Saint)   1   1
1   1   Catneride Plunkett
Edward Plunkket   1

1700

1
William Plunkett   Sarah
       Cordis
1   1

Nancy Purvis   Ruben Plunkett
1   (Fought in Revolutionary War
1   - was wounded).
1   1

1
Nancy Plunkett   Mr.
       Dowden

1800

1   1
1
Hiram Rees   Nancy Plunkett Dowden
(Fought in Civil War)   1
1   1

1
Nanette Rees   Joseph Martin Skain
1   1

1900

1   1
1
Chester Bernard Bunte (Father)   Helen Skain (Mother)
1   1
1   1   1   1   1
Helen Bunte   1   William Skain Bunte   1   Patrick Bunte
Nanette Bunte   John Joseph Bunte

2000

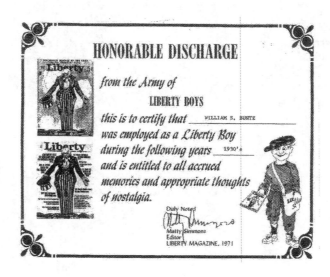

Chapter 2

Junior High

I started Sidney Lanier Junior High School in Houston, Texas when I was 12 years old in 1935. I loved sports, and got on the track team. Because of my height, I did well, especially in the high jump. I enjoyed school and received good grades.

The only other thing I remember about Junior High was my English teacher. If you didn't answer her question correctly, she would throw a book at you! And this was a public school!

High School

I went to Lamar High School in Houston, Texas (1938-1940).

I took all the science and math courses I could get. I also was on the football and track teams. High school football was much different back then. There were no offense teams and defense teams then. Each player played both offense and Defense. (60 minutes). Also, in Texas, there were no professional teams. All High school games were played at night, and 20,000 to 40,000 people came to each game! The lights were so strong that once the game started, the players didn't realize that it wasn't daylight. Even though I was on the football and track teams, I was able to stay on the National Honor Society each year, with God's help!

During the summers, between high school years, I was able to go to Colorado and work on my uncle's ranch, livery stable, and filling stations. They were located at Grand Lake, Colorado (next to the Rocky Mountain National Park). For about two weeks, I would help harvest his hay crop at his ranch (heavy manual labor). The rest of the summer, I would round up his 25 horses in his pasture and "drive" them the two miles to my uncle's stable early each morning. At the end of the day I would "drive" them back to the pasture on horseback. During the day, I had several jobs. The main one was to clean the stable and horses, saddle up the horses, and then take groups of people on trips in the Rocky Mountain Park. Some trips were only an hour or two, and some were several days. The horseback trails went as high as 10,000 feet. The rest of the time I was filling cars with gas at one or both filling stations. One was next to the stable, and the other one was across the street.

During the last week or two of the summer, I would take a hiking trip up in the mountains with a local friend. One time we hiked about nine miles to the base of Mt Baldy (12,500 ft.) We then climbed the mountain and slept on top. The next day we climbed down and hiked back to the town of Grand Lake.

One year my friend Stanley Morris drove up to Grand Lake with me for the summer. Stanley used to hunt snakes on the outskirts of Houston, and I would help him. All four poisonous snakes in the US (rattlesnake, copperhead, water moccasin and coral snake) were located in the Houston area, along with dozens of non-poisonous types. He would ship these live snakes to zoos and

Lamar High School

Bunte leads as Moe and Paul look on.

Mirabeau B. Lamar Senior High School
Houston, Texas

Hereby Awards The Letter

to Billy Bunte

In FOOTBALL   Year 1954

I am on the way to High School Prom.

Junior High school track team (I am on bottom right).

collectors all over the United States. I learned a lot about snakes (for example where to step, and where not to step, when hiking in the woods, the different types of snakes, and which were poisonous and which were not). Each type of snake was different. If you tried to catch or you startled a hognose snake, for example, he would raise his head and make believe he was a cobra. If you still went after him, he would roll over and play dead. After you left, he would turn back over and hide in the bushes. I saw Stanley get bitten by a rattlesnake once. He just took out his snake bite kit, cut an "X" on each fang-hole with a razor, and used a special suction cup to suck the poison out of the bite. He didn't go to a doctor or hospital, and didn't have any reaction to the bite. I am no longer afraid of snakes, but I do respect them.

After we worked all summer for my uncle, we took a hike up to the continental divide (12,000 to 14,000 feet high). At night we would climb down to timberline about 11,500 feet to cook dinner and to sleep. We hiked about 50 miles along the top of the continental divide, and hiked back to Grand Lake. It took about one week for the entire hike.

At the cabin where my uncle lived, we had a fireplace but no central heating, and it was cold at night, even in the summertime. Another one of our jobs was to cut firewood for the fireplace and wood stove. There was also an "outhouse" - all the comforts of home!

My uncle paid Stanley and me each $1/day for our work. This would be equivalent to $9/day at today's money value.

When I was in high school, I became interested in homing pigeons. I built a large screened "fly" plus enclosed nesting shed. As a school English project I wrote a book called "Raising Pigeons from Experience."

At that time you could buy a baby alligator through the mail from Florida. I sent for one and built a small pen and pool. I called him "Snaggletooth." One day he escaped and we never found him. Many years later we heard about a large alligator in a small river near our house!

I had a "dark room" in the basement of our house. I was able to develop and print all the photos that I took. It was fun and it saved me some money!

My book (front cover)

Stanley with snake in sack on belt

Snaggletooth

I used to go hunting with my father in southwest Texas. Mostly we would hunt wild ducks and deer. One trip was to the "King Ranch," which is the largest ranch in the United States. My father knew the owner. We quietly approached a very large lake that had many ducks sitting in the water. When we got close, all the ducks started flying. My father and I both shot with our shotguns, and missed. The ranch owner took out his six shooter and with one shot, he killed two ducks! We would also hunt deer there. The ranch was so large the main problem was getting lost!

The summer before I went to college, I worked at the Houston Shipbuilding Corp. as a welder's helper. The ships being built were Liberty Ships. They were designed to carry supplies and cargo for the army and navy. The welder I was working with was welding in an enclosed area called the "double bottom" (four feet from top to bottom). This was on the very bottom of the ship where the fuel oil is to be stored. At that time the welding rods were coated with asbestos, so the area where we were working in was always full of asbestos smoke. The dangers of asbestos were not known at that time. I was really blessed that I have no signs of asbestos.

Results of deer hunt (Left to right - My father, myself, brother Jack, and uncle Arnold.

Uncle Harry's ranch.

Uncle Harry's gas station & riding stable.

Grand Lake (Mount Baldy in back ground).

Top of Mount Baldy showing area where we slept (12,500 feet elevation).

Friend on top of Mt Baldy, cooking and eating in bed (on a bed of rocks!).

On the way back to stable (we took the horses up to 10,000
feet and then climbed the rest of the way to top)

I am looking back at Grand Lake (1.5 miles wide and 5.5 miles long) from top of Mt Baldy)

I am looking at other mountains from top of Mt Baldy.

View from continental civide showing three small lakes at 9,000 feet (center of photo).

Top of glacier (just below continental divide).

Stanley looking at map on continental divide.

Stratalayers visible in cutaway of Mt Alice. (Stanley in photo).

Top of Mt Alice (14,000 ft). Photo taken at 12,500 ft.

I am on the continential divide (12,000 ft) looking at other mountains. Note the "sea fossils" in foreground!

A small pond with fish at 10,000 ft.

Stanley and I cutting wood for the cabin.

Chapter 3

College

I wanted to be an engineer, so I tried to get in the best engineering school in Texas, Rice University. The founder of Rice, William M. Rice, was a very wealthy oil man. He was actually able to have a tuition-free university. The only problem was that the scholastic requirements were very high. Fortunately my high school record was such that I was able to be accepted with the help of a letter of recommendation written by an oil man who was a good friend of my father.

The hazing of freshmen was very bad. We had to wear a "Freshman Hat" so the upper classmen knew who to pick on. One night a group of us were in a large room with what looked like the football team. One requirement was that we repeat a string of profanity. I refused. I had never used any before and I decided that I wasn't going to start then. I then was forced to run the "gauntlet." I couldn't sit down for a few days after that!

The first year of engineering school was the same for chemical, electrical, mechanical, and civil. By the beginning of the second year, I decided to go for a degree in chemical engineering. In order to graduate from Rice, it was necessary to pass a spelling test of over 100 words. Spelling was not one of my best talents! I took the test and did not pass. You could keep taking it each year, but you had to pass it by the end of your senior year, or you could not graduate. Because I was so busy with my other classes and activities, I put off taking this spelling test until I was taking my final exams in my senior year! I stayed up all night before the test, and with quite a few prayers, I actually passed. If I had missed one more word, I would not have graduated! (You had to get 90 out of 100 correct...)

During the summer vacation between the first and second years at Rice, I worked with a company that took soil samples at a depth of 12 feet in a grid pattern over a large area. They tested the samples and found they could estimate the amount of oil that was present, and at what depth. The samples were obtained with a 5" diameter hand augar. Two of us would turn the augar until the hole was 5 feet deep. Then we would unscrew the handle, screw another 5 foot pipe to the end of the original pipe, reattach the handle, and dig another 5 feet. The soil sample would be removed from soil inside the auger and the sample placed in a special container with the location marked on the jar. We would then cut by hand all the brush between the first hole 300 feet down to the next hole. A transit would be used to make sure the next hole was in the right direction from the first hole.

KIPLINGER'S
PERSONAL FINANCE MAGAZINE

Private Colleges
Worth *the* Price

SEPTEMBER 1999

Private Colleges
Worth *the* Price

Top-ranked Rice University attracts high-caliber students, and costs a third less than the Ivy League schools.

When is a prestigious school a great value? When it's affordable, too.

What?! A college survey that doesn't put Harvard, Princeton and Yale at the head of the list? Welcome to *Kiplinger's* first review of private universities, where to make the cut a school must pass both academic and financial tests.

Last September, we highlighted public colleges and universities that provide top-quality education at an affordable cost. This year, we looked for gems among the nation's 1,600 private schools, once again putting ourselves in the shoes of parents who want excellence for their children but who also care how much it costs.

Perched at the top of our list of 100 great values: Rice University, in Houston. The Owls can boast a high-caliber student body, top-notch faculty, small classes and sky-high graduation rates (see the table beginning on page 100). Ivy League schools can claim the same attractions, of course, but here's the clincher: A year at Rice cost about a third less last year, at $21,500 for tuition, fees, room and board. And Rice guarantees freshmen that their tuition in the future will rise no faster than the rate of inflation: This year's seniors pay $13,200 in tuition, instead of the $15,350 charged entering freshmen.

It gets even better. More than a third of students received a merit scholarship from Rice last year (for academic achievement, musical talent or leadership ability, for instance). For them, the average annual cost was about $18,000. The school also awarded $6.3 million in need-based scholarships (plus a couple of million in loans and work-study opportunities). The average student with financial need paid just $5,456 per year out of pocket and owed a little more than $12,000 in education loans at graduation—significantly below the 1998–99 average of $16,000 for all the private colleges in our survey.

By Kristin Davis

Rice University's Ranking

The Profile from Rice University was as of January 1994 - (see the next page).

William Bunte

Association of Rice Alumni
William S. Bunte.

Spouse: Lorna

Children: Pamela, Nannette, David, Donna, Linda

Grandchildren: Leah and Mark.

Education after Rice: Course in Factoring at Open University (Orlando, Florida) - passed certification program.

Brief History: Lt. Jg - U.S. Navy during WWII in Pacific (including Okinowa Invasion and Tydhasn) on repair ships. Career: Mostly management positions in large and small companies, Owner of several small businesses including conveyor manufacturing, solar heating, Real Estate and Factoring. Active in several Technical and business associations. Traveled to Japan, European Countries and South and Central America, Canada and Alaska.

Retirement: None, still working.

Achievements: Happy 47 years of marriage.

Interests: Would like to travel, but also would like to spend time and money helping those less fortunate than I have been.

A brief personal statement on the influence of Rice Institute on your life: Helped prepare me for the technical and business world. Most of all it helped me think in an organized way.

What would you have done if you had not attended Rice? I can't imagine.

See previous page.

The holes were all in a designated grid pattern. The person working with me was 6' 5", 300 pound Rice football player. He said this was the hardest job, physically, that he had ever worked at. We did this all summer. At the end of the summer, I proposed to the company owner, a method of eliminating cutting the brush between the holes. It involved the use of a portable direction finder and other portable electronic equipment. I went into the Navy after that summer, and never did find out if they tried my suggestion.

While I was at Rice, I dated several girls, mostly to school dances. They were all very nice, but none that I would desire any serious relationship with, that is, except for Mary Lou... Had I not been sent to midshipmen's school in New York City, where I met my first wife (to be), and I had come back to Houston after the war, things might have been different. About thirty years after the war, I came to Houston on business, and decided to see if Mary Lou or her mother were still around. I went to her old house and knocked on the door. Her mother opened the door and with a big smile and said "Billy Bunte!" (In Texas almost all William's were called Billy instead of Bill). I didn't think that she would even remember me. I only met her once when I came to pick up Mary Lou to go to a dance. I asked her how Mary Lou was doing. She said she is doing fine - she is married and has 12 children!

I joined the Navy at the beginning of my third year at Rice. At that time, the Navy had taken over most of Rice with their "V-12" program. This program allowed you to graduate, but then you had to go to a midshipmen school for officer training. Besides our regular engineering classes, we now had navy classes and other activities. Our typical day would start (5 AM) with calisthenics, marching, running, obstacle course, etc, and then classes on seamanship, rope knots, etc. Then we would have breakfast, followed by our regular engineering classes and labs for the rest of the day. After dinner, we would have time to study. My roommate was very, very smart. He could read something once, and he would remember it for months. Not me. I would have to read and study the same thing many, many times, before I knew it... These were long hard days for me.

We had no time-off or vacations. We worked spring, summer, fall, and winter. On February 22, 1944, I actually did graduate with a degree in chemical engineering, and was sent to midshipmen school in New York City. There were several other midshipman schools at different locations, but seven of us from Rice went to New York.

Some Navy friends after graduating from Rice (Bill Davis - best friend - top left, I am top center).

From Rice senior year book.

SENIORS

BUNTE, WILLIAM SKAIN   Houston
    B.S. in Ch.E.
    Honor Roll '41, '42: Engineering Society;
    American Chemical Society; Rally Club;
    Ave Maria Club; Intramurals

Chapter 4

Midshipmen School

After I graduated from Rice (February 22, 1944), I took the train from Houston to New York City. I had never been there before, so I looked forward to seeing it. We came under the Hudson River, and underground to the subway station. I then transferred to another subway that took me to Columbia University. I didn't even see the New York skyline! The midshipmen school was at Columbia. I checked in, registered, and along with everyone else, was immediately restricted for one month! The "Deck" midshipmen would live in the Columbia dorms, and the "Engineering" midshipmen would be on the old battleship "Illinois", which was tied up on the Hudson River, just below Columbia. The main reason the potential engineering officers were on the ship was that the engine room equipment was still there and could be used in the instruction of its operation. We were kept very busy with daily drills, exercises, classes, standing watch, cleaning, exams, etc.

There were about 600* midshipmen on the Prairie State (Old Battleship Illinois). It was very crowded, especially before breakfast in the "head" (bathroom). It was one large room with no partitions and no privacy!

One day a group of midshipmen put on a show just for the men on the ship. There were various acts, but the best one was when one midshipman went through all the uniforms we wore each day. First he came from behind a partition in his PJ's, then he went back behind the partition, and within 3 seconds he was back in his track suit, then back behind the partition and out again in 3 seconds dressed for classes, etc. throughout the rest of the day. Each time he came out, he would explain what the uniform was used for. At the end he came out and took a great applause. He then called out a name, and his twin brother came out from behind the partition! They were in different divisions, so we never saw them together.

After the first 30 days restriction, we had liberty on some weekends. On the first liberty available, I went to a dance at Barnard College (women only). I was looking at the various girls dancing, when I noticed a girl jitterbugging. She tripped and fell to the floor. She immediately got up and continued dancing.

FOREWORD

ON the pages following is recorded the passage of the Eighteenth Class through this training school. Fifteen hundred American young men are tested, shaped and tried, and they prove their fitness to join the ranks of this nation's Navy as officers of the line.

Our training for four months has sown in our minds the seeds of Naval leadership. As we go out on the seas, may these fundamentals grow and prosper, to make us capable, courageous leaders. May we never lose our faith that the ways of force and greed are not those of our country nor its people — that tolerance and integrity and truth will forever be held to as "right."

To the end that these ideals be preserved, our country is at war. For the day when peace returns we are willing to fight; that our children may never know war, we are willing to die. . . .

I am on date with Lorna (while still a Midshipman).

I then started dancing with her (Lorna). She was very nice, beautiful and a lot of fun. We hit it off right away. I asked her for a date for the next Saturday and each available Saturday until I graduated. I asked her to go to my graduation dance. Her girlfriend, Helen, asked if I could find a nice midshipman to take her to the dance. I picked out a midshipman, Don, who seemed nice. After graduation I went overseas for almost two years. During that time Lorna and I wrote letters to each other almost every day. Don and Helen married after the war and now have five children!

There were about 2000* Midshipmen at the start, and only about 1500 graduated and became officers.

Prairie State (converted Battleship Illinois)

---

*   Includes both "Deck" and "Engineering".

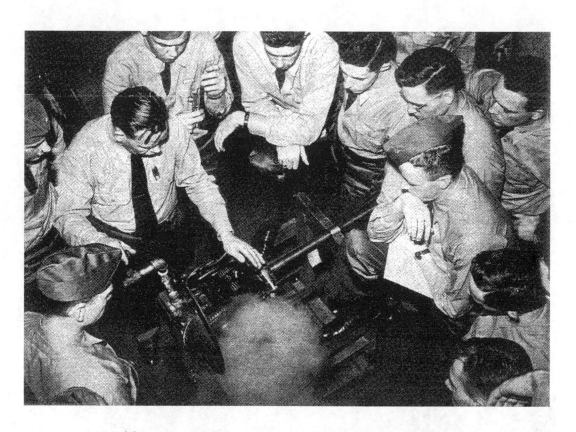

Midshipmen at a class on equipment in the ships engine room.

WILLIAM ADAMSON, JR.
331 Fishers Road,
Bryn Mawr, Penn.
Princeton University

LEE T. ADAMSON
331 Fishers Road,
Bryn Mawr, Penn.
Princeton University

Identical twin actors in Midshipmen show.

... "Wahr is hell!"

My Day

As A Distinguished Lady Columnist *Might* Lead It

Prairie State, Thursday. — I came aboard after flying to New York from Madame's Country home outside Melanesia and travelling uptown on the Van Cortlandt subway with a very interesting gentleman on his way to 145th Street who told me of the housing shortage on upper Riverside Drive.

The officer-in-charge met me at the gangway and took me below to the wardroom for breakfast, which I understand these Navy men term "mess." The little midshipmen were just arising, a horn was blowing, and I heard one of them saying to his mates in a distinctly Louisiana accent, "Whar is hell." I found myself agreeing with him, although I never did have an opportunity to discuss it with him.

No sooner had we finished our scrambled eggs and turned to discussing the appalling conditions among crowned heads of the Balkans than the midshipmen were doing push-ups on the drill deck. Our fighting men are fit, there is no doubt of that.

After the exercise period, the men put on a few more clothes, and I was permitted to wander about the old ship. I saw plenty of soap and water in the "heads", as they call the . . . . er . . . and the men were doing very well although, as I have always asserted, cleanliness is difficult to maintain at the front.

There were many things on the officers' program for me. I shook hands with several of the crew in the engine room, and one boy from Texas gave me the name of his girl friend, whom I will look up when I visit El Paso. Then I climbed atop the mainmast and saw the view up and down the Hudson. Fresh air gives one an exhilarated feeling.

A nice young ensign was conducting a class in turbines and motors and we stood along the bulk-heads for awhile watching him. Many of the midshipmen commented as the lesson progressed and asked questions, which is only right, after all, for even in the Navy, free speech is our right.

The morning over, our party had lunch with the Second Platoon. I spent a very interesting fifteen minutes while the Platoon Leader told me that seven of the twelve men in his group preferred hot oatmeal to Whesties, even in this warm weather, and I made a mental note to mention this to Mr. Forrestal at our next meeting.

Later in the afternoon we noticed a large group of midshipmen in the lounge studying, and it seemed to me that this showed an admirable interest on the part of our Youth. Literature will build America. The officer who conducted the tour of the ship told me of an interesting anecdote connected with his own training. He was detained twenty-seven minutes by taking the 180th Street Express when reporting back from liberty one Sunday, and was given thirty demerits and guard duty on the bridge deck for six cold nights. I understand this is a rather widespread practice in the Navy.

There was a formal inspection late in the day, and the black shoes all had plenty of polish and the white caps glistened. A lieutenant told me that the cap covers are removable and cost a dollar and thirty cents apiece.

I could not wait for the evening meal, in spite of my anxiety to see how that roast beef which I could smell all day turned out, but I had an appointment to address the WAVES at Cooks and Bakers School at Hunter so I had to request permission to go ashore. This accomplished, I left the wonderful old PRAIRIE STATE just as the watch officer was seeing that all the midshipmen were in for the night.

It was most nautical, but in a way I am rather glad my day is done!

I was permitted to wander about the old ship. I saw plenty of soap and water. cleanliness is difficult to maintain at the front.

white caps glistened. A lieutenant told me that the cap covers are re-

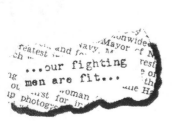

...our fighting men are fit...

cleanliness is difficult to maintain at the front

Me (3rd from left), Don (far right), and four other former midshipmen
waiting (fishing!) in Florida before joining their ships.

Me as an Ensign
(After Midshipman school).

Lorna and me and Don and Helen just after I graduated from Midshipmen school (June 1944).

Lorna & me and Don & Helen (1987) - Still best friends.

Chapter 5

U.S. NAVY

After I graduated from midshipmen school on June 24, 1944, I was sent to the sub chaser school in Miami, Florida until my ship the USS Mona Island (ARG-9) was completed.

While I was waiting for the ship to be completed, I took flying lessons at a seaplane base in the New Jersey Meadowlands. I actually learned on a seaplane! I completed the lessons, and was ready to solo, when I had to leave and go to my ship, and report for duty.

The Mona Island was a repair ship and could repair just about anything. It had everything from a watch repair shop to a foundry, plus the spare parts required. The ship was almost two football fields long, and we had 600 men, plus 32 officers on board. The outside and the engine room were very similar to the ship I worked on at the Houston Shipbuilding corp. Much of the below deck part was different because of all the repair shops located there.

The Mona Island was commissioned on October 17, 1944 at Baltimore, Maryland. I reported to the ship on that date. We then went to Norfolk Naval Base to complete the fitting operation and shakedown of the ship. On December 2, 1944, we went to Guantanamo, Cuba. On December 11, we left Guantanamo, and went through the Panama Canal headed to San Diego, California.

I didn't realize at the time, that this was a combat area. I read a book, after the war, and discovered that over 300 ships were sunk by German submarines along the same path we had taken from Norfolk to the Panama canal. There were also Japanese submarines on the Pacific side. And we went unescorted. This was kept quiet at the time because there were not enough Navy ships available at that time to escort all the ships in that area.

We had two days of "R and R" at San Diego, California. Five of the officers invited me to go to Tijuana, Mexico on liberty with them. We looked at various sites in the city. Then they went into what looked like a hotel. When we got inside, it was obvious that it was a "house of ill repute."

I walked out and waited for them for some time. It was very difficult to do, since I was hoping to make some officer friends on the ship. However, God's friendship came first. I did find other officer friends later on the ship that had good morals, and we became good friends.

After our layover in San Diego, we left to go to Hawaii. About half way to Hawaii, around midnight, our radar picked up a friendly airplane. All of a sudden it disappeared on the radar screen. The location was entered in the ships log, but since there was no distress signal, the captain said not to stop.

(101b
/CBOP/P16-4/AH/V-7
558-69-68

824 Niels Esperson Bldg
Houston, Texas

September 29, 1942

From: Officer-in-Charge.
To :   BUNTE, William Swain, A. S. V-7(G), USNR.

Subject: O R D E R S.

1.   Having this date been enlisted as an apprentice seaman in Class V-7, U. S. Naval Reserve, you will return to your home to await further orders for active duty training.

2.   You are informed that you have become a member of the Naval Service of the United States and that you are subject to military discipline at all times. All orders issued by competent authority will be obeyed promptly. Correspondence must be answered immediately up on receipt. All communications with the Navy Department which you may deem necessary must be forwarded to the Commandant, EIGHTH Naval District, Federal Office Building, New Orleans, Louisiana.

3.   Until you are called for active training duty you will keep the Commandant's Office informed of your correct mail address. You have given as your address the following: 1936 Canterbury, Houston, Texas.

PRESTON MOORE.

My enlistment.

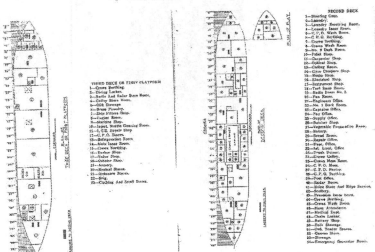

U. S. S. MONA ISLAND
(A. R. G. 9)

☆

The U. S. S. MONA ISLAND *was built by Bethlehem Fairfield Shipyard, Inc., Baltimore, Maryland.*

The keel was laid April Tenth, Nineteen-Hundred and Forty-Four, and the Ship was launched-May Eleventh, Nineteen-Hundred and Forty-Four and delivered to the Navy May Twentieth, Nineteen-Hundred and Forty-Four.

Conversion for use by the Navy was accomplished at the Key Highway Plant of the Bethlehem Steel Company, Baltimore, Maryland.

The MONA ISLAND is named after an island in the Caribbean Sea. This island lies East of Porto Rico in the center of the Mona Passage to which it gives its name. To mariners Mona Island is a familiar landmark.

USS MONA ISLAND (ARG-9)
OFFICERS

☆

COMMANDER KENNETH F. HORNE, USN, *Commanding Officer*
LIEUT. MICHAEL A. DONOHUE, D-V(G), USNR, *Executive Officer*

LT. COMDR. RAYMOND J. SMITH, DC-V (G), USNR
LIEUTENANT FRANCIS J. VERVILLE, D-V (G), USNR
LIEUTENANT JAMES C. MCCONAHAY, E-V (S), USNR
LIEUTENANT SAMUEL N. DAVIS, E-M, USNR
LIEUTENANT JOHN B. PAYNE, D-V (G), USNR
LIEUTENANT WALTER E. GREENE, C-V (S), USNR

LIEUTENANT JOHN J. FOWLSTON, USN
LIEUTENANT THOMAS BADGER, D-V (S), USNR
LIEUTENANT HENRY W. OHRENBERGER, MC-V (G), USNR
LIEUTENANT GEORGE G. NEICE, SC-V (G), USNR
LIEUTENANT FRANK W. HYDE, DC-V (S), USNR
LIEUTENANT FREDERICK A. STOCK, ChC-V (S), USNR
LIEUT. (jg) ARTHUR G. AXTELL, D-V (G), USNR
LIEUT. (jg) EMERSON C. MEYERS, D-V (S), USNR
LIEUT. (jg) DANIEL ROYER, CC-V (S), USNR
ENSIGN ALPHA R. HARRISON, USN
ENSIGN PAUL R. NELSON, USN
ENSIGN FRANK E. SCHROETER, D-V (G), USNR
ENSIGN PAUL V. BLAKE, D-V (S), USNR
ENSIGN JAMES F. HACKETT, E-M, USNR
ENSIGN MILTON L. DUVALL, E-M, USNR
ENSIGN WILLIAM S. BUNTE, E-V (S), USNR
ENSIGN PETER V. CIGNETTI, E-V (S)
ENSIGN JOE A. DUFFEL, SC-V (G), USNR
BOATSWAIN HOMER N. ANDERSON, USN
GUNNER WALTER H. COLEMAN, USN
CARPENTER WILLIAM J. CONNERS, USN
ELECTRICIAN FREDERICK M. SPINNEY, USN
RADIO ELECTRICIAN CHARLES E. REED, E-V (S), USNR
MACHINIST JOHN C. CURCHOE, E-V (S), USNR
MACHINIST JOHN KIER, USN
MACHINIST WILLIAM G. MILLER, USN
PAY CLERK DAVID C. LASSITER, USN

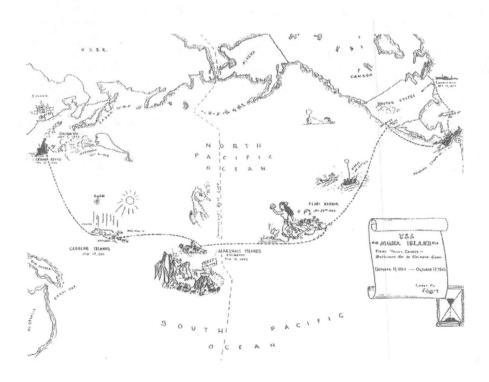

The next morning, we received word that a US army plane went down, and that all ships in the area should search for it. They gave the approximate location. Since we knew the exact location, the captain decided to turn around and look for any survivors. Because of the large waves in the area, it was hard to see anything in the water. After many hours of searching, we finally saw the life raft. It was a difficult rescue because of the high waves, but five Army Air Corpsmen and a dog were finally brought aboard our ship. They were a very happy group!

After two days in Pearl Harbor, we went to various islands. At the Marshal Islands, we had liberty on one of the small islands with warm 3.2 beer, and relaxed (?) in the hot sand and hot sun. All of the palm trees had been knocked down during the battle for this island group. However, this liberty was a change from our regular routine aboard ship.

My division included about 250 men in the Repair Department. One day seven of the younger mechanics asked me if I would teach them calculus. I had just finished a course in calculus at college, so it was fresh in my mind. I said I would teach them if they would teach me how to operate all the machines on the ship (lathes, milling machines, drill presses, etc.) and they did!

The Caroline Islands were the staging area for the invasion of Okinawa. There were thousands of navy ships of all kinds - as far as you could see in all directions. While we were there, we saw our first kamikaze (suicide) plane hit an American hospital ship that was close to us. In an invasion, the minesweepers must go in before the landing, to remove any mines. Since the Mona Island was primarily a repair ship for the minesweepers, we had to be at Okinawa at the same time as the sweepers.

We were at Okinawa during the entire campaign (April 1, 1945 to August 15, 1945). There were over 3,000 kamikaze planes that attacked U.S. and British warships during this battle. There were 5,000 US Navy personnel killed, and 4,800 wounded. Sixty three destroyers, 13 aircraft carriers, 10 battleships, and 5 cruisers were either sunk or badly damaged.

Our ship was at "General Quarters" (battle stations) or repairing damaged ships for most of our time at Okinawa. We were at General Quarters anywhere from 1 to 24 hours at a time. So we didn't have much time to sleep or eat. My battle station was in the engine room, so I couldn't see any of the action. However, I was able to tell something by our ship's guns. When the 5 inch went off, I knew that the enemy plane was very high above our ship. When the 3 inch fired, and then the 40 mm, I knew the plane was diving towards us.

UNITED STATES SHIP
MONA ISLAND
ARG-9

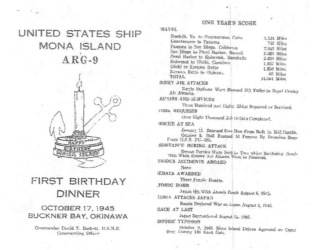

**FIRST BIRTHDAY
DINNER**

**OCTOBER 17, 1945
BUCKNER BAY, OKINAWA**

Commander David T. Baskett. U.S.N.R.
Commanding Officer

ONE YEAR'S SCORE

TRAVEL

Norfolk, Va. To Guantanamo, Cuba	1,124 Miles
Guantanamo to Panama	740 Miles
Panama to San Diego, California	2,843 Miles
San Diego to Pearl Harbor, Hawaii	2,285 Miles
Pearl Harbor to Eniwetok, Marshalls	2,400 Miles
Eniwetok to Ulithi, Carolines	1,257 Miles
Ulithi to Kerama Retto	1,250 Miles
Kerama Retto to Okinawa	65 Miles
TOTAL	11,964 Miles

ENEMY AIR ATTACKS
Battle Stations Were Manned 213 Times to Repel Enemy Air Attacks.

REPAIRS AND SERVICES

Three Hundred and Eighty Ships Repaired or Serviced.

WORK REQUESTS

Over Eight Thousand Job Orders Completed.

RESCUE AT SEA

January 17, Rescued Five Men From Raft in Mid-Pacific.

October 9, 1945 Rescued 51 Persons By Breeches Buoy From U.S.S. PC-590.

ASSISTANCE DURING ATTACK

Rescue Parties Were Sent to Two Ships Suffering Bomb Hits While Enemy Air Attacks Were in Progress.

SERIOUS ACCIDENTS ABOARD

None.

MEDALS AWARDED

Three Purple Hearts.

ATOMIC BOMB

Japan Hit With Atomic Bomb August 6, 1945.

RUSSIA ATTACKS JAPAN

Russia Declared War on Japan August 8, 1945.

PEACE AT LAST

Japan Surrendered August 15, 1945.

HISTORIC TYPHOON

October 9, 1945 Mona Island Driven Aground on Coral Reef During 140 Knot Gale.

KAMIKAZE AIR ATTACK AT KERAMA RETTO (OKINAWA)
MAY 1945

Picture taken from USS Mona Island as the marines landed at Kerama Retto (Okinawa).

When the 20 mm fired, I knew the plane was almost on us. This happened one night when our flagship (one with the admiral on it) started firing at the plane with tracers (when we were down to firing our 20 mm guns). The plane immediately turned away from us and followed the tracers down to the flagship. Twenty-nine men on the flagship were killed and many injured. God was watching out for us that night, actually every night and day, because ships were being hit all around us all the time!

Another problem was the Jap torpedo boats. These were small speed-boats with a small torpedo attached to the front of the boat. These boats were hidden in caves at the shore water line. At night, they would come out of the caves and head for the U.S. ships anchored there in the harbor. Most fortunately, we were able to destroy them before they could ram us.

We were also blessed in having the Catholic chaplain on our ship. The number of Catholic men going to daily Mass (when possible) increased dramatically during the Okinawa battle. The chaplain also gave a service for the non-Catholic men, and the number also increased during the battle.

The war with Japan ended on August 15, 1945. I think everyone on our ship was very happy. We had been scheduled to go in on the invasion of Japan in a few weeks, and everyone knew that the casualties would be very high on both sides (over 1,000,000 soldiers).

We were at Okinawa during the typhoon season. When the weather forecaster in the Navy predicted that a typhoon could hit our area, as many ships as possible would go out to sea to try to miss it. One time Admiral Halsey's Task Group of many ships ended up in the middle of a typhoon. Three destroyers sank along with all the men aboard. On October 9, 1945, a typhoon was supposed to pass by Okinawa, so all the ships stayed in port. The "eye" of the typhoon came right over the part of Okinawa where all of the ships were anchored! We clocked the wind at 185 MPH. We had both anchors out and the engines going full speed ahead to take the strain off the anchors. The anchor chains were made of two inch thick steel. Both anchor chains snapped from the high winds, and we were set adrift. The radar was not working because of the high winds, so we were not able to locate the entrance to the harbor. We ended up on a reef and started to break up because of the sharp rocks in the reef and the high winds. The captain announced on the ships PA system to prepare to abandon ship. Fortunately, he decided against it, because you could not live in the water, with high wind and rain. We could see many dead bodies floating in the water. I was supposed to go out on a deck to try to fix a piece of equipment. I had a rope tied around my waist and the other end tied to the ship. One of the sailors on our ship told me later that I had saved his life. Evidently he went out on deck to retrieve something, but without a rope. He was about to be blown into the water.

MINE SQUADRON 15 (1)

U.S.S. DOUR (AM223) - Flagship

MINE DIVISION 43			MINE DIVISION 44			MINE DIVISION 45		
AM225	ELUSIVE	(F)	AM224	EAGER	(F)	AM240	HAZARD	(F)
AM226	EMBATTLE		AM223	DOUR	(FF)	AM241	HILARITY	
AM351	ADJUTANT		AM232	EXECUTE		AM242	INAUGURAL	
AM352	BITTERN		AM233	FACILITY		AM286	REFORM	
AM364	GRAYLAG		AM234	FANCY		AM287	REFRESH	
AM365	HARLEQUIN		AM235	FAXITY		AM288	REIGN	

MINE SQUADRON 20 (1)

U.S.S. ELLYSON (DMS19) - Flagship

MINE DIVISION 58			MINE DIVISION 59			MINE DIVISION 60		
DMS24	FORREST	(F)	DMS19	ELLYSON	(FF)	DMS29	BUTLER	(F)
DMS25	FITCH		DMS20	HAMBLETON		DMS30	GHERARDI	
DMS26	HOBSON		DMS21	RODMAN		DMS27	JEFFERS	
DMS23	MACOMB		DMS22	EMMONS		DMS28	HARDING	

CONFIDENTIAL

The USS Mona Island repaired the DMS-22 (Emmons). It was hit

I must have tied my rope to him and got him back inside the ship. I didn't remember it at the time. I guess I was so engrossed in fixing that piece of equipment, but I finally did remember later.

There was another ship (a PC*) that was on the same reef as our ship, and they were starting to break up. There wasn't anything we could do until the wind came down some. When it got down to about 75 mph, we shot a rope line over to them, and then rigged a breeches buoy between the two ships, and started pulling the men on the PC over to the Mona Island, one at a time. It took 2 hours and 20 minutes to get all 51 men off the PC and onto the Mona Island. The captain of the PC was the last one to be rescued. Just as he reached the Mona Island, The PC split and sank. There were 140 ships that were either sunk or badly damaged.

After the typhoon was over, we had to wait until the tide was high enough for an ocean-going tug to pull us off the reef. They then pulled us with everyone on board, to Guam where there was a dry dock large enough to hold our ship. The steering gear was damaged so badly that a jury rig was made up so the ship could be steered from the fantail (rear end of the ship). Because of that, our maximum speed was 6 knots. It took us approximately two months to go from Guam to New York Shipyard to complete the repair on the ship!

Assembly for the transfer of original Captain and installation
of new Captain on the USS Mona Island

---

* Patrol Craft (PC)

A friend and me at Okinawa.

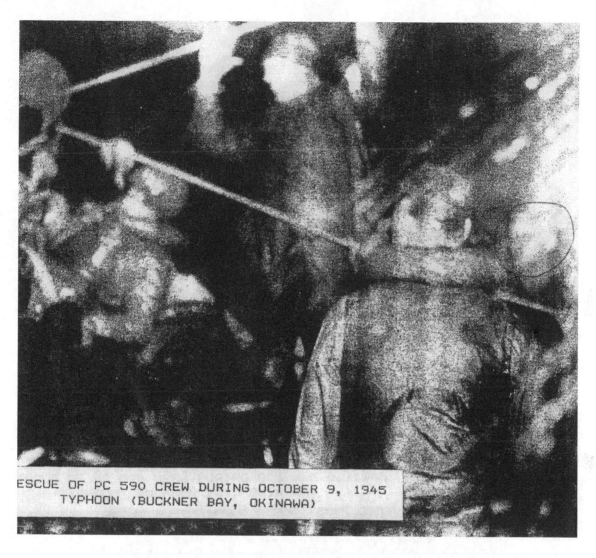

ESCUE OF PC 590 CREW DURING OCTOBER 9, 1945
TYPHOON (BUCKNER BAY, OKINAWA)

The circled area on the right side of this photo is me. (I just happen to remember that I was at that location right next to the ship's doctor).

Damage to 24" diameter mast from typhoon.

TRAILS END for this Coast Guard ship came during an Okinawa typhoon.

SAVED FROM THE TYPHOON'S FURY

FROM the early October typhoons that struck Okinawa, devasting the island base, have come many dramatic stories of men against the sea. One of the most thrilling was that recounted by the commander of a Coast Guard patrol craft who, along with his entire crew, was saved from his doomed craft in a hairbreadth rescue at the height of the storm.

Heroes of the rescue were the men of the Navy repair ship, the USS *Mona Island*, who fought to save six officers and 45 men of the Coast Guard vessel, although the intense gales and mountainous waves made operations hazardous.

Arriving in Buckner Bay with 15 men from a destroyer for transfer to the Navy Receiving Unit at Okinawa, the 173-ft. Coast Guard craft *No. 590* hurriedly discharged its passengers and headed for shelter in an area known as Baten Ko. Once at the shelter area, the *590* settled down to sweat out the storm, but shortly before noon the anchor chain, taut from the constant strain, broke.

Running with the storm, the *590* zigzagged to avoid other ships distressed by the typhoon. Finally, the vessel was driven onto a reef, but hung there for only a few minutes before plunging on to another reef a mile away. This time it was grounded fast, stranded with engines and communications dead.

Pounded mercilessly by the gale and the heavy seas, the *590* had just begun to buckle amidships when the *Mona Island*, barely visible because of the storm, loomed ahead. A collision seemed inevitable but the repair ship stopped barely in time with a scant 50 feet to spare.

Rescue operations were begun immediately, although the heavy seas threatened to sweep the men from the decks which were made additionally hazardous by gear crashing crazily about. The breeches buoy was finally cleared and the first man left the distressed Coast Guard patrol craft at 1755.

Two hours and 20 minutes later, the last man, Lt. Comdr. Charles R. Pool, USCGR, skipper of the Coast Guard vessel, started the tortuous trip to the *Mona Island*. Just as he reached the repair ship, the *590* split and sank.

Taken from Navy magazine "All Hands".

I am in the center, with two Jap P.O.W's, and two repair men from my Division (on Okinawa).

The U.S. Navy bore the brunt of kamikaze fury off Okinawa during the desperate battle to secure the island

The ferocity of the fight between ships and planes that occurred off Okinawa in April and May 1945 is unparalleled in modern military history.

While a three-month battle raged on land between 100,000 troops of the Japanese Thirty-Second Army and 172,000 American GIs and Marines, the U.S. Navy remained on station to lend supply, air support and naval gunfire to the effort to secure the island as a staging area for the invasion of the Japanese homeland. All the while, these American ships and crews were exposed to an enemy of the most fearsome kind—one bent on self-destruction as well as the destruction of its foe.

Waves of kamikaze aircraft sortied against the U.S. vessels in an effort to force them back from Okinawan waters. In mass attacks known as *kikusui*, or "floating chrysanthemums," Japanese pilots hurled themselves against the fleet. More than 7,000 American GIs and Marines died on Okinawa (see related story, P. 25). Offshore, the U.S. Navy lost nearly 5,000 sailors killed and 4,800 wounded. A total of 13 destroyers and one destroyer escort went to the bottom, while 13 aircraft carriers, 10 battleships and five cruisers were heavily damaged. Nearly 50 more destroyers and destroyer escorts were damaged. Ships large and small were kamikaze victims. Two of the most tragic, and at the same time heroic, stories of the naval battle off Okinawa are those of the fleet carrier *Bunker Hill* and the destroyer *Hugh W. Hadley*.

No strangers to combat, *Bunker Hill's* 3,000 crewmen remembered a close call at the Battle of the Philippine Sea when a Japanese bomb had splashed perilously close by and caused slight damage to the ship. The 27,000-ton Essex-class carrier had been launched on December 7, 1942, exactly one year after the Pearl Harbor attack.

Vice Admiral Marc A. Mitscher, commander of U.S. Task Force 58, flew his flag aboard *Bunker Hill* on May 11, 1945. That

After taking several hits from Japanese suicide planes on May 11, 1945, the U.S. Navy carrier Bunker Hill burned for 24 hours, but her determined crew managed to get the fires under control.

morning, 30 planes were armed and fueled on the flight deck while 48 more were being readied on the hangar deck below. The vessel's aviation fuel and ammunition stores had been replenished just the day before, and nearly 2 million gallons of fuel oil sloshed in her tanks.

At 10:05 a.m., a Japanese Mitsubishi A6M2 Zero suicide plane came in low out of a cloud bank on the starboard beam, crashing into the parked planes on the flight deck. Less than a minute later, a second kamikaze roared from above in a near vertical dive and crashed at the base of the carrier's island, its 550-pound bomb ripping a 40-foot gash across the deck. Instantly, *Bunker Hill* became an inferno. A great cloud of black smoke erupted from the ship, mixing with super-heated steam from ruptured valves. The ship's top three decks were blazing from amidships to the fantail. Stunned sailors gathered their wits to man hoses and battle flames. Crewmen trapped aft by the fires fought for their lives.

Captain George A. Seitz made two crucial decisions that probably saved his ship. Seitz ordered the stricken carrier to be turned broadside to the wind so that the smoke and flames did not run the vessel's full length.

He also ordered an abrupt degree turn, causing thousands of gallons of water that been used to fight fires and mable fuel to spill over B Hill's side and into the sea.

Damage control parties f the flames with great her many falling with hoses in when overcome by smoke hours after the first kami hit, the fires aboard *Bunk* were under control. The co high—396 seamen dead o ing and another 264 wo *Bunker Hill* then turned from the battle, towar haven of Ulithi Atoll, miles away.

USS *Hugh W. Hadle* been commissioned in N ber 1944, a swift new de equipped with the latest nology. Off Okinawa sl one of many small warships that pulle on the picket line in one of several de rings to provide early warning of inc Japanese aircraft and protect suppli

On the same spring morning *Bun* had won its desperate struggle to s *Hugh W. Hadley* was on picket duty tion 15. It was early when the kan came. During that long, dreadful da than 150 suicide planes assaulted H *Hadley* and her sister ship USS *Evan* an hour between 8:30 and 9:00, H gunners knocked a dozen enemy from the sky.

Then, at 9:05, a Yokusuka "Baka"—in essence, a rocket-p flying bomb—laden with explosive little destroyer squarely. *Hadley* th hits from a bomb and another kami rapid succession. A third kamikaze l seemed to seal her fate. Her skippe mander Baron J. Mullaney, ordered abandoned. A skeleton crew re aboard, and in a 30-minute mira wounds were temporarily patched. lost 28 men, and 67 of her cre wounded, but the ultimate triumph *W. Hadley* was a testament to the the U.S. Navy crewmen.

I finally made it by the end of the war!

The last battle, the bloodiest battle

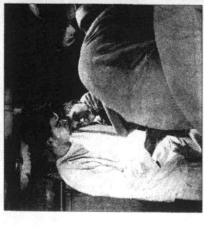

The invasion of Okinawa was massive and bloody. Among the Marines, 7,163 were killed and almost 32,000 wounded, while the Navy sustained 9,713 casualties on ships. More than 107,000 Japanese and Okinawans were killed. Here, a Marine private has his wounds dressed on a hospital ship en route to Guam from Okinawa.

NATIONAL ARCHIVES

From the caves of Okinawa to the skies above, the Japanese fight with furious desperation

BY WILLIAM GORDON
FOR THE STAR-LEDGER

Among Kenneth R. Williams' souvenirs of World War II is an envelope filled with metal scraps, kept in a drawer in his Rockaway home.

The handful of bits and pieces of scorched aluminum and steel is all that's left of the suicide plane that crashed into his destroyer, the USS Gregory, during the Battle of Okinawa.

One piece, an engine part, is punch-marked with what appears to be the design of a chrysanthemum, a revered flower in Japan, but here a manufacturer's symbol.

By coincidence, Kikusui ("floating chrysanthemums") was the Japanese code name for the 10 successive waves of kamikazes sent against the American invasion fleet

The kamikazes — "divine wind" — would help make the battle that began Easter Sunday, April 1, 1945, the longest and most costly in terms of men and ships in the history of the U.S. Navy.

The attack on the fleet also would include suicide boats and piloted rocket-propelled flying bombs called ohka — "exploding cherry blossom."

It was stubby-winged ohka, with a human guidance system and 2,000 pounds of high explosives, that plunged into a destroyer, USS Mannert L. Abele, sinking it in five minutes, with 81 dead and 32 wounded.

The American force of 1,600 ships with 545,000 Marines and GIs on board was mightier than the Allied armada on D-Day at Nor-

island as a staging area for the invasion of Japan's home islands, but it proved to be the last battle of the war in the Pacific.

Combined with the fighting on land, Okinawa achieved ranking as the greatest land-sea-air battle of all time.

And yet, owing to the magnitude of other world events that bracketed the battle — along with delayed release of casualty figures — the Okinawa campaign did not capture the attention of the home front that other major battles did, according to veterans.

We didn't get much attention back home, said Edward "Buzzy"

Edward "Buzzy" Fox of Union was a 6th Division Marine in the Okinawa invasion. "There were screaming dogfights above, kamikazes crashing into ships and artillery fire I couldn't tell was 10 miles or 10 yards away. I was scared. And just miserable," he said. Fox is holding a frame containing the U.S. flag, the wartime Japanese flag and a crucifix from a destroyed church in Naha, Okinawa.

ED MURRAY/THE STAR-LEDGER

who fought in the savage battle for Sugar Loaf Hill on the island, the costliest in Marine Corps history, claiming 2,662 killed and wounded.

There were many reasons why Okinawa didn't garner much attention: The war had already ended in Europe, President Roosevelt died while the battle was being fought and the atom bomb was dropped a little more than a month after the battle ended.

Fox, a longtime basketball coach at St. Patrick High School in Elizabeth, said he had arrived in May and was rushed as a replacement to Sugar Loaf Hill. He recalls being frightened and miserable and at one point being in rainwater up

Kenneth R. Williams of Rockaway was on the destroyer USS Gregory off Okinawa when it was attacked by Japanese kamikazes. Luckily, a bomb from a kamikaze that made it through withheld.

JERRY MCCREA/THE STAR-LEDGER

JAPAN SURRENDER AUGUST 15, 1945 ON USS MISSOURI

The final proof that I no longer in the navy.

The final proof that I
no longer in the navy.

55

President of the United States of America.

To all who shall see these presents, greeting:

Know Ye, that reposing special trust and confidence in the Patriotism, Valor, Fidelity and Abilities of _____ WILLIAM SAIN HUNT _____ I do appoint him

A LIEUTENANT (JUNIOR GRADE)

in the Naval Reserve of The United States Navy to rank from the _____ day of _____ He is therefore carefully and diligently to discharge the duties of such office by doing and performing all manner of things thereunto belonging.

And I do strictly charge and require all Officers, Seamen and Marines under his Command to be obedient to his orders. And he is to observe and follow such orders and directions from time to time as he shall receive from me, or the future President of The United States of America, or his Superior Officer set over him according to the Rules and Discipline of the Navy.

This Commission to continue in force during the pleasure of the President of the United States for the time being.

Done at the City of Washington this _____ SECOND _____ day of _____ DECEMBER _____ in the year of our Lord one Thousand Nine Hundred and _____ FORTY-NINE _____ and of the Independence of The United States of America the One Hundred and _____ SEVENTY-THIRD _____

By the President:

398885
Relative Precedence from 1 January 1946

HEADQUARTERS OF THE
COMMANDANT THIRD NAVAL DISTRICT
FEDERAL OFFICE BUILDING, 90 CHURCH STREET
NEW YORK 7, N. Y.

From: Commandant THIRD Naval District
To:

Subj: Honorable Discharge from the U. S. Naval Reserve

Ref: (a) SecNav ltr dtd 27 May 1955

Encl: (1) Your Officer Service Record (NavPers 3021)

1. In accordance with provisions of reference (a), your honorable discharge from the U. S. Naval Reserve was effected on 1 September 1955.

2. In accordance with current instructions, service records of officers who are discharged from the U. S. Naval Reserve are to be forwarded to the officer concerned. Accordingly, enclosure (1) is forwarded to you for your retention. Please be advised that enclosure (1) is merely an administrative file and does not contain a complete record of your service. Your complete file is maintained in the Bureau of Naval Personnel, Washington 25, D. C.

3. You are requested to return to the Commandant your Naval Reserve Identification Card in the self-addressed envelope which is enclosed for your convenience. If you do not have an Identification Card in your possession please state reason. Attention is invited to the fact that this card is not to be confused with your Certificate of Satisfactory Service (NavPers 556) which you should retain.

By direction

Lieutenant (jg) William S. Hunt,
USNR

To you who answered the call of your country and served in its Armed Forces to bring about the total defeat of the enemy, I extend the heartfelt thanks of a grateful Nation. As one of the Nation's finest, you undertook the most severe task one can be called upon to perform. Because you demonstrated the fortitude, resourcefulness and calm judgment necessary to carry out that task, we now look to you for leadership and example in further exalting our country in peace.

THE WHITE HOUSE

THE SECRETARY OF THE NAVY
WASHINGTON

August 30, 1946

Dear Lieutenant (jg) Hunt:

I have addressed this letter to reach you after all the formalities of your separation from active service are completed. I have done so because, without formality but as clearly as I know how to say it, I want the Navy's pride in you, which it is my privilege to express, to reach into your civil life and to remain with you always.

You have served in the greatest Navy in the world.

It crushed two enemy fleets at once, receiving their surrenders only four months apart.

It brought our land-based airpower within bombing range of the enemy, and set our ground armies on the beachheads of final victory.

It performed the multitude of tasks necessary to support these military operations.

No other Navy at any time has done so much. For your part in these achievements you deserve to be proud as long as you live. The Nation which you served at a time of crisis will remember you with gratitude.

The best wishes of the Navy go with you into your civil life. Good luck!

Sincerely yours,

James Forrestal

Lt. (jg) William Sain Hunt
Decelle St.
_____, Mississippi

67

NOTICE OF SEPARATION FROM U. S. NAVAL SERVICE
NAVPERS-553 (REV. 8-45)

1. SERIAL OR FILE NO.	2. NAME (LAST) (FIRST) (MIDDLE)	3. RATE AND CLASS/OR	5. PLACE OF SEPARATION
RANK AND CLASSIFICATION	4. PERMANENT ADDRESS FOR MAILING PURPOSES		USNPSC, Camp Shelton (Rt. 60) Norfolk, 11, Va.

359367 BUNTE, William Skain
Lt. (jg) E(L)   USNR
404 Decelle St.
Jackson, Mississippi

6. CHARACTER OF SEPARATION
Released From Active Duty-HONORABLE

7. ADDRESS FROM WHICH EMPLOYMENT WILL BE SOUGHT
Same as No. 4

8. RACE	9. SEX	10. MARITAL STATUS	11. U.S. CITIZEN (YES OR NO)	12. DATE AND PLACE OF BIRTH
W	M	Single	Yes	5-2-23, Lexington, Ky.

13. REGISTERED	14. SELECTIVE SERVICE BOARD OF REGISTRATION	15. HOME ADDRESS AT TIME OF ENTRY INTO SERVICE
YES ☐ NO ☒	- - - - - - - -	1936 Canterbury St., Houston, Texas

RECORD OF NAVAL SERVICE

16. MEANS OF ENTRY (INDICATE BY CHECK IN APPROPRIATE BOX)

☒ ENLISTED   DATE 9-29-42
☐ INDUCTED   DATE
☒ COMMISSIONED   DATE 6-29-44

17. DATE OF ENTRY INTO ACTIVE SERVICE	18. NET SERVICE (FOR PAY PURPOSES) (YRS. MOS. DAYS)
7-1-43	3-9-23

19. PLACE OF ENTRY INTO ACTIVE SERVICE
Houston, Texas

20. QUALIFICATIONS, CERTIFICATES HELD, ETC.
Division Off., Ass't Engineer Off., Ass't Repair Off., Repair Off., ARG-9

21. RATINGS HELD
A.S., Mid'n, Ens., Lt. (jg)

22. FOREIGN AND/OR SEA SERVICE WORLD WAR II
☒ YES   ☐ NO

24. SERVICE (VESSELS AND STATIONS SERVED ON)
U.S.S. Mona Island (ARG-9)

23. SERVICE SCHOOLS COMPLETED	WEEKS
USNRMS, N.Y., N.Y.	15
V-12, Rice Inst., Houston, Texas	32
Fire Fighting, Norfolk, Va.	1
Pre. Comm., Newport, R.I.	8

PAY & INSURANCE DATA

IMPORTANT: IF PREMIUM IS NOT PAID WHEN DUE OR WITHIN THIRTY-ONE DAYS THEREAFTER, INSURANCE WILL LAPSE. MAKE CHECKS OR MONEY ORDERS PAYABLE TO THE TREASURER OF THE U. S. AND FORWARD TO COLLECTOR'S SUBDIVISION, VETERAN'S ADMINISTRATION, WASHINGTON 25, D. C.

25. KIND OF INSURANCE	26. EFFECTIVE MONTH OF ALLOTMENT DISCONTINUANCE	27. MO. NEXT PREMIUM DUE	28. AMOUNT OF PREMIUM DUE EACH MONTH	29. INTENTION OF VETERAN TO CONTINUE INS.
NSI	June	July	6.50	Yes

30. TOTAL PAYMENT UPON DISCHARGE	31. TRAVEL OR MILEAGE ALLOWANCE INCLUDED IN TOTAL PAYMENT	32. INITIAL MUSTERING OUT PAY	33. NAME OF DISBURSING OFFICER
$ 348.80	$ None	$100.	J.G. HAGSTROM, Cdr. USN Ret.

34. REMARKS
Released-Points, Certificate of Satisfactory Service No. 95618. Issued. American Campaign Medal, Asiatic-Pacific Campaign Medal, World War II Victory Medal.

35. SIGNATURE (BY DIRECTION OF COMMANDING OFFICER)

J.J. Mac Leod

J.J. MAC LEOD, Lt. Comdr. USNR
Civil Readjustment Officer

EMPLOYMENT AND EDUCATIONAL DATA

36. NAME AND ADDRESS OF LAST EMPLOYER
Maintenance Engineering Corp.
Houston, Texas

37. DATES OF LAST EMPL'MT.	38. MAIN CIVILIAN OCCUPATION AND O. O. T. NO.
FROM May 1943 TO July 1943	Student (Chem. Engineer)

39. JOB PREFERENCE (LIST TYPE, LOCALITY, AND GENERAL AREA)
Chemical Engineer
New York

40. PREFERENCE FOR ADDITIONAL TRAINING (TYPE OF TRAINING)
Undecided

41. NON-SERVICE EDU. (YRS. SUCCESS. FULLY COMPLETED) GRAM. 8 H.S. 4 COLL. 4	42. DEGREES	43. MAJOR COURSE OR FIELD	44. VOCATIONAL OR TRADE COURSES (NATURE AND LENGTH OF COURSE)
	BS, Ch. E.	Chem. Eng'r.	None

45. RIGHT INDEX FINGERPRINT

46. OFF DUTY EDUCATIONAL COURSES COMPLETED
- - - - -

MILITARY EXEMPTION ALLOWED
BORO OF RIVER EDGE, N. J.
AUG 17 1959

47. DATE OF SEPARATION	48. SIGNATURE OF PERSON BEING SEPARATED
7-21-46	*William Skain Bunte*

CERTIFICATE OF APPRECIATION

It Is Hereby Proclaimed That The Citizens Of
The State Of New Jersey Declare Their Deep Gratitude
& Appreciation To

VETERAN WILLIAM S BUNTE

**In Recognition Of Proud & Unselfish
Military Service In Defense
Of The United States Of America.**

Thomas H. Kean, *Governor, State of New Jersey*

Chapter 6

Married Life

First Marriage:

    After almost two years of writing letters to each other, Lorna and I got to know each other pretty well and knew that we were in love. After I was discharged from the navy and had a job, I asked her to marry me, and she said "yes!" I wanted her to meet my parents. I had already met hers. So we took a train to Jackson, Mississippi, where my parents were currently living. Lorna and my parents got along great, and we had a very nice visit. We even went horseback riding, Lorna's first, but she did really well!

    I rented a room in a private house in Bound Brook, NJ, and lived there until I could find an apartment for us to live in after we were married. I couldn't afford a car at that time, but I was able to get a ride to work with a fellow employee who lived nearby. With all the men coming back from the war, it was very difficult to find an apartment for us after we were married. I finally found one in Highland Park, NJ. It was truly a "one" room apartment. At one end of the room there was a sink, a small stove, a small table, and a small refrigerator. In the middle of the room sat a small sofa and a lamp. At the other end of the room, there was a true "Murphy Bed" that went up into the wall, a small bureau, and a small closet. Very cozy!

    Lorna was a Lutheran, so we had to get married in the Catholic rectory. It was a small wedding, with just Lorna's parents, her sister and brother-in-law, and Lorna and I. Her parents took us out to dinner, and we spent the night at the Roosevelt Hotel in New York City. The following morning we left on our honeymoon for Quebec Canada by train. We stayed at the Chateau Frontenac in Quebec City. There were many excellent restaurants there and the prices were lower than in New Jersey (and very much lower than today, but so were the wages!). At one restaurant I forgot where we were and ordered a US bottle of wine. When I saw the bill, I realized that it was "imported" with a price to match! We did a lot of sightseeing in the area, including the shrine of St. Anne de Beaupre.

When we returned home, I had to buy a car (7 year old Pontiac) in order to get back and forth to work. With my new job, I had to work rotating shifts (one week days, next week 4 PM to 12PM, following week 12PM to 8 AM, etc.). It wasn't the best for those just married! But we managed, because it only lasted for four months during my training period at work.

After a few months, we were able to get on a list for a garden apartment development (Brookside) that was being built in Somerville, NJ. They finally gave us a date that we could move in. We told our present landlord that we would move out by that same date. When we moved into the new apartment, we found that it wasn't finished.

Menu from restaurant in Quebec, Canada - note prices!

Chateau Frontenac where we stayed in Quebec City

Certificate of Marriage

Church of

Our Lady of Refuge
2721 Bainbridge Ave.

This is to Certify

That _William A. Bunte_

and _Lorna E. Pitz_

were lawfully **Married**

on the _2_ day of _June_ 19_47_

According to the Rite of the Roman Catholic Church

and in conformity with the laws of the State of

New York , Rev. _EP Gallagher_

officiating, in the presence of _Jeremiah Hurley_

and _Helen Doherty_ Witnesses, as appears

from the Marriage Register of this Church.

Dated _June 2, 1947_

EP Gallagher _asst._
Pastor.

NO 212 © D. P. MURPHY CO., NEW YORK

Lorna and I on my return from the Navy, and before our marriage.

The hot water heater wasn't working, and there was no water. The only thing that worked was the electric. Lorna went home to her mother's and father's house in New York City. I had to stay because I had to go to work. I had to bring water in with a bucket, and heat the apartment with electric appliances (toasters, electric irons, etc. which didn't help much, so I bought a small electric heater). This lasted for two weeks, and then Lorna came back from NYC. Our first child was born in 1948. We then needed another bedroom, so we moved into a two bedroom apartment in the same complex.

Most of the people who moved into Brookside Gardens at the same time were about our age, and the husbands (and some wives) had just been discharged from the armed services. We made several close friends there, playing bridge, and taking trips together. We still get together occasionally.

In 1952, we moved into our first house - a small two bedroom split level in Plainfield, NJ. Plainfield was very nice in those days before the "race riots". Some of our friends from Brookside also moved in the same area. Between my job and all the upkeep of the house and yard, I was very busy.

When our daughter, Pam, was two years old, we drove to Lexington, Kentucky, to visit my grandmother, and other relatives of my mother. We enjoyed our visit, and Lorna got to meet some of my relatives. On the way back home, we were driving through West Virginia on a two- lane highway. When we reached the top of a hill, we saw another car coming towards us in our lane! I didn't even have time to put on the brakes. The other car crashed into us head-on. We were going about 35 mph, and the other car at least that fast. The steering wheel broke in my hands and cut my arms. Lorna sprained her ankle very bad, and Pam broke the windshield with her head. In those days, there were no seatbelts in cars, and all children seats were in the front seat. The car was "totaled" and we were taken to the hospital. We were in the hospital for one week, and then took the train back home. In spite of the injuries which healed, we were blessed by God that we were not killed!

As our second and third children came along, we needed more space, so we moved to a larger house only three blocks away. It was much larger with six bedrooms! We really didn't need that many, but the price was right, and we did expect more children. It was a three story colonial with high ceilings, a fireplace, and large rooms. This meant very high heating and air conditioning bills! The wiring was the old "tube and knob" and needed to be replaced. I decided to re-wire it myself, because we couldn't afford to hire an electrician. I did one area at a time, but it seemed like it took forever.

Lorna and Pam leaving the hospital.

Car after accident.

Somerset County Holy Name Society

First house (Plainfield, NJ).

Board of Governors
1968-1969

COPPERMINE SWIM CLUB

President: Walter Cronkright
34 Claire Dr., Somerville
722- 1091

Vice President: Edward G. Socher
640 Foothill Rd., Somerville
722- 2903

Secretary: Mrs. Jack Cardozo (Ginny)
775 Sunset Ridge, Somerville
725- 2822

Treasurer: Kenneth T. Garty
775 Hardgrove Rd., Somerville
722- 3571

→   William S. Burke
8 Brian Drive, Somerville
722- 4189

James A. Gibbons
12 Claire Drive-East, Somerville
722 9643

Local swim club.

In 1959, I decided to change jobs to one in Rochelle Park (in north Jersey). The company was Print-A-Tube. (See Business Life).

As much as we hated to move out of our six bedroom house in Plainfield, we felt it was too far a commute. We moved to a three bedroom house in River Edge, NJ, which is very close to Roselle Park. Our friends Don and Helen also lived in River Edge.

I never asked, or even hinted to Lorna that she should consider becoming a Catholic. I tried to set a good example, and prayed that God would make it happen, if that was his will. Unknown to me, Lorna started taking instructions in the Catholic faith at the local church in River Edge. She became a Catholic on Easter Sunday 1961! We had a great life together. I guess all marriages have some problems. We did have a little trouble communicating with each other. We heard about this group called "Marriage Encounter" that was supposed to solve that problem, so we went on a Marriage Encounter Weekend. The leaders would give a teaching and then each couple would discuss it and then write a letter to each other on their feelings about the teaching. None of this was shared with the other couples. One main point was that feelings are neither good nor bad. That means that you should never get mad or upset at any feelings your spouse shares with you. We were also supposed to have a meeting with just the two of us once a week to discuss any of these feelings. All of this did help our communications with each other.

I will never forget one home improvement job around the house, and there were many. It was when I decided to insulate the attic floor. It happened to be a very hot summer day, and the insulation was the loose type. Between no shirt, perspiration, and the insulation, I felt as if I had a thousand needles digging into me. I learned the hard way!

I started my first vegetable garden at this house. It was about eight feet by ten feet in size, and I learned a lot about which ones grew the best and the best soil for them.

One evening I learned a lot about lightning. I was standing at the backdoor during a big storm and I saw a huge lightning bolt hit a 24 inch diameter tree in our back yard. The tree was 100 feet from the back of the house. The lightning actually started at the base of the tree, and threw the tree all the way up to the house! It didn't actually hit the house, but it was thrust within a few feet. I had heard that lightning can start at the ground and then go up, but this was the first time that I had seen it.

After living in River Edge for two years, I received a great job offer back in the Somerville area from Egan Machinery.

We then moved to Bridgewater (near Somerville) to a "colonial" style, four bedroom new house. With one acre of land, I was able to add some extras that I had always wanted, such as a large outdoor patio, a rock garden with a waterfall and a small pond, and a large vegetable garden (four times as big as the one in River Edge).

Menu cover showing Guy Lombardo's signature (top left).

It took a lot of evenings and weekends, but it was fun making them. I used various types of fertilizer in the vegetable garden (horse manure, cow manure, and chicken manure). One day we went to pick up some chicken manure at a chicken farm. I put it in boxes in the car trunk. On the way home our youngest daughter Linda, three years old at the time, said "I thmell thumping"!

Our daughter, Pam, loved horses. She and I used to go to the local riding stable and ride for hours. She had a favorite horse called "Chickie" that was quite spirited, but Pam could handle her. Our son David and daughters Nannette, Donna and Linda also loved to go horseback riding. We all used to go together when we were at our cabin in the Poconos.

Whenever Lorna and I wanted to celebrate a special occasion, with dinner and dancing, we would go to the Roosevelt Hotel where Guy Lombardo was playing at that time. One night he even signed our menu.

In 1975, we went on a Marriage Encounter trip to Europe with about 800 other Marriage Encounter couples from all over the US. We flew over to France in a chartered 747 plane and landed in Lourdes (the only time a 747 had ever landed there). The runway was so short that the plane could only take off if it had no passengers and very little gas.

Lourdes was a wonderful religious experience. We went to a beautiful Mass in an underground church. I heard of one healing in our group, in the special bathing pool, but I didn't know the person that was healed. We also said the rosary at the Grotto where Mary appeared to the children. This rosary was special to me because of the location, but also because it was ALL in English (There were no "thees and thous"). I never did like those Old English expressions, so since that experience at Lourdes, I have been saying the rosary the way we said it at the Grotto. Note: Most Bibles now are the same-(See Matthew 6: 9-13).

We went from Lourdes to Rome on a special train hired just for our Marriage Encounter group. Since 1975 was a special Holy Year, there was a lot going on in Rome such as opening the special doors to St Peter's church. We also were able get a close-up look at Pope Paul XI.

We also went on a pilgrimage to the Holy Land with Father Joe Neville who gave Lorna and me the Spiritual Exercise (see the chapter on "Spiritual Life - Retreats" for details). We went with 40 other Catholics. A pilgrimage is much different than a Tour.

Our cabin in the Pocono's, and our sail boat.

The bear that followed me back to our cabin.

We would see people from a Tour walk into one of the special shrines, look around, and walk out. When we went to the same shrine, Father Joe would read a chapter of scripture that referred to this location, and then he would say Mass there. We were also blessed to be in Jerusalem on Good Friday and Easter Sunday. Even then there were problems with the Arabs. On Easter Sunday we were just coming out of the old city, when there were people shooting all around us. I found out later that an Israeli soldier had shot an Arab in the "Temple of the Dome." One Arab, trying to run away from the shooting, ran into Lorna, almost knocking her down. We ran to a Catholic church that was nearby and stayed there for four hours, until the shooting stopped. Even with that incident, it was a very spiritual pilgrimage.

When our son, David was living and working in Anchorage, Alaska, we took a cruise from Seattle, Washington to Anchorage. We saw all kinds of whales, fish, and special birds on the way. We also made several interesting stops along the way.

We had a great visit with David. He hired a small airplane to fly us to see Mt McKinley, the highest mountain in North America. On the way, I mentioned to the pilot that I had taken some flying lessons. He let me sit in the co-pilot's seat and fly the plane until we reached Mt McKinley at a height of 20,320 feet. He said I did very well.

One day when I was at work, I started feeling a pain in my chest. It didn't feel serious, but I called my doctor just to be sure, and he said that he would meet me at the hospital emergency room. When I got there, the pain was much worse. The monitor on the wall showing my heart beats, which I could see, was going crazy. The doctor said I was having a heart attack! While he was working on me, one of the nurses called my wife at home. She gathered two of our daughters who happened to be at home, and they prayed for my recovery, and then came to the hospital. By the time they came, I was in ICU and feeling fine. The doctor could find no damage to my heart and nothing that would indicate that I had a heart attack. He couldn't explain it! In the weeks that followed, I had three different stress tests, and none showed any damage to my heart. During one of these tests they were increasing the speed of the treadmill, and also elevating it. It got to a point where my head touched the ceiling. They stopped the treadmill, and took the ceiling panel out, and resumed the test. My head ended up in the space above the ceiling! Even though the doctor couldn't explain my complete, rapid recovery, we knew that it was the prayers that did it!

Lorna and I joined The People of Hope, a Charismatic community, in 1983.

BUNTE FAMILY REUNION AT BILL'S BROTHER PAT'S RANCH IN COLORADO

Road leading to Pat's ranch.

Everyone at the reunion

My brother Pat

My brother Jack and his son David at reunion.

I am returning with others from a hike on the ranch.

My sisters Nanette (left) & Helen (right).

Award for Best
Producer

BILL BUNTE

For Producing and
Acting In the 1993
classic "Bunte Follies"

Award during family reunion

Award during family reunion

Children playing games at reunion

When I worked for Egan Machinery (see Business for more information.), I was able to take Lorna on some very interesting trips. At the time I was a sales enginer, and did a lot of traveling. My teritory was the whole world. At the time, we were flying First Class. My boss said I could also take my wife, if I purchased two tourist tickets instead of one First Class. Egan had licensees all over the world. I was able to take her on a two week trip to Japan, with hotel, food, and air fare paid by the company. The licensees even had a guide take her sighseeing while I was working! We also took trips to England, Sweden, Finland, Denmark, Germany, and France - paid for by the company.

We also went on a pilgrimage to Medjugorje (See the section on "The People of Hope").

I went to Jury Duty several times. One time at Somerville, NJ, I was selected to serve on a malpractice case (A woman vs her doctor). There were six men and six women on the jury. When all the presentations were given, I was convinced that the doctor was not guilty. I had been appointed forman of the jury by the judge. As we deliberated, five of the women, and one man felt the doctor was guilty. The rest believed the doctor was not guilty. We kept discussing this for hours, and still couldn't get anyone to change. Then out of the blue, I heard this voice very clearly " Get them to pray..." I didn't even know if that was legal, but it could only be God or His messenger that said it . I got everyone's attention and told them that we weren't getting anywhere, and would they object if we said a prayer to help us. They finally said O.K. So I prayed "Lord you know who is right and who is wrong in this trial, please give us the wisdom to vote the correct decision". We discussed the case for ten minutes, and then voted. All twelve of the jurers voted that the doctor was not guilty!

We had a group of very good friends (twelve couples) that we called the "Dinner Bridge Group". We would get together at one of the couple's home once a month for dinner, and we would play Bridge for a few hours after we ate. The host couple would rotate each month to a different couple. None of us were expert Bridge players, but we had a lot of fun. One of the problems with getting older, is that all of these friends, and many others, have either moved to southern states or have died.

In 1989, I had to go the hospital because of a twisting of my colon. It required an operaton to remove two feet of my colon. In 1990, adhesions from the above operation caused a blockage in my small intestine. I was rushed to the hospital at about 7 PM. The Emergency Room doctors ran all kinds of tests, but could not find the cause of the pain. The pain became unbearable but the

ASBURY PARK PRESS

IO. 87   ASBURY PARK, N.J., MONDAY, APR. 12, 1976   36 PAGES

Mr. and Mrs. Ray O'Brien of Englishtown welcome approximately 7,000 persons to the Ocean Grove Auditorium for a
marriage encounter Mass yesterday. The hall was decorated
with banners in English and Spanish proclaiming love.

Asbury Park Press

First in Auditorium
7,000 Attend Ocean Grove Mass

By G.L. VAN RENTHUYSEN
Press Staff Writer

OCEAN GROVE. — Peace
and love filled every cubic
foot of the Ocean Grove
Auditorium yesterday as
approximately 7,000 persons,
most of them Catholics,
attended Mass.

According to George J.
Hergesheimer, president of
the Camp Meeting Associa-
tion, this is the first time the
auditorium was used for a
Catholic Mass since the
community was founded in
1869.

Hergesheimer, who with
his wife attended the four-
hour ceremony, said no residents of this predominately
Methodist community
objected to Catholics using
the hall for religious pur-
poses. The affair was
approved by the association's
Board of Trustees.

"Catholics are just as
Christian as Protestants
and we're all Christians," he
said.

The second annual Palm
Sunday rally was sponsored
by the World Wide Marriage
Encounter Movement. Par-
ishioners and clergy of the
Diocese of Trenton and Pat-
terson and the Archdiocese of
Newark took part, said coor-
dinators Jerry and Donna
Peterson.

During the Mass couples
renewed their marriage
vows while priests and nuns
repeated their religious vows
and renewed their commit-
ment to the church.

Marriage Encounter, a
program started by the the
Roman Catholic Church to
help make good marriages
better, is not designed to
help marriages in trouble.
Through various meetings
and weekend encounters

couples are expected to learn
more about themselves and
each other. It is not limited
to Catholics.

Archbishop Peter L. Gerety
is celebrated the Mass following a 15-minute audio-
visual presentation of a
recent American marriage
Encounter pilgrimage to
Lourdes and Rome.

We Have Only Just
Begun was the theme for
the annual rally which last
year was held in Convention

Marriage Encounter Mass
(We were out there somewhere!).

REACH OUT
Worldwide Marriage Encounter

AS I HAVE LOVED YOU   JOYFULLY PUBLISHED FOR THE LOVERS OF METUCHEN AND TRENTON DIOCESE

Dear Lovers,

We are filled with excitement and anticipation for
our Marriage Encounter movement as we progress in
our time of formation. This formation had it's
beginnings in the living room sessions a few years ago
thinking as what we as couples remembered of our
original weekend, why or why not we became involved and why we dialogued or didn't.

The Leadership Conferences going on around the
world are a result of that input. The recognition is
that all of us who have made a weekend are formed
by others who share our experience in positive / or
negative ways we form who are today and where we
as a movement will be going.

Convention 1982 "So the World May Believe"
takes right off on that same input and asks us to look
at our own self image and how much we really need
to believe in the goodness of who we are that "God
does not make junk" is true and that we must
honestly and openly look at our self worth and believe
in who we are.

Dearest Lovers,

We would like to share and additional dimension we have added
to our relationship by dialogueing on scripture.

It all started when we were blessed this spring by going on a
Pilgrimage to the Holyland during Easter week. Now, when we do
scripture dialogue, we can visualize Jesus actually being in the
countryside with real people. Our feelings are much more
authentic, and we learn more about how each of us feel about
various moral teachings and events in the life of Jesus. It certainly
adds a very real and wholesome spiritual dimension to our
relationship.

It is not necessary, however to go to the Holyland in order to have
rewarding scripture dialogues. There are some devotional
pamphlets and books with scripture passages and very good
meditations and pictures of the Holyland. one excellent pamphlet
"Where Jesus Walked" can be obtained by writing (no charge or a
small donation) to: Sacred Heart League, Walls, Mississippi
38680.

The introduction to this pamphlet starts off "Come, dear Friend
in Christ, Come on a prayerful, pictorial pilgrimage. Come and
see an ancient land, experience the holy place, come walk where
Jesus walked. Walk awhile with Him, remember, and relive thirty
poignant, salvation events. As you walk where Jesus walked, our
prayer is that you will draw closer to Him so that you may live
even more in His great love".

This is our prayer for you too, but also so that you will at the
same time grow closer to each other.

We Love You,
Bill & Lorne Bunte

From Marriage Encounter newsletter.

doctor and nurses said that they were under orders not to give me any medicines for the pain because of other tests they had planned for the next morning. I offered this pain up to Jesus, because I felt this pain was something like what He suffered for my sins. After 15 hours (10 AM the next morning), the doctors ran a barium enema test. I could watch on the TV-like monitor. When the barium reached my small intestine, it flooded into my abdomen! The doctors rushed me to the operating room. I asked if I could see a priest. They said there wasn't time. While I was on the operating table, I could hear the doctor say, "He is in shock, I think it is too late to operate." The anesthesiologist said, "His blood pressure is too low to operate." Fortunately, they did decide to operate anyway. I found out the next day that when they operated, the doctor found that fourteen feet of the small intestine had ruptured and was all black. My abdomen was full of the contents of the intestine. After the operation the doctors all said it was a real miracle that I lived. Evidently, God had other plans for my life!

In 1993, we had a reunion of the entire family and relatives (a total of 40 persons). It was held at my brother's ranch in the Rocky Mountains of Colorado. It was the first time that our extended family had ever gotten together, and the last because they are not all still alive. We showed many of the home movies that my father had taken when we were growing up. This brought back many great memories. We also played games with the children, and went on long hikes in the mountains. The ranch was set at an altitude of 10,000 feet.

In 1993, we found that my wife, Lorna, had cancer of the uterus. The doctors tried chemo and other medicines, but nothing helped. She died on February 28, 1994. We had a great marriage of 46 years. She had the last rites before she died. She was a very strong Christian, and a wonderful person. I am sure she went right to heaven!

Lorna was an accomplished artist. She painted with both oils and water colors, and won many awards. We have some of her paintings in our townhouse, and my children have some of her paintings too.

We had five children, and I am very proud of all of them. Pam is the oldest. She is a professor and anthropologist at California State University Long Beach, and a widow. She also works with various Indian Tribes to get them recognized by the U.S. Government so that they can get financial aid. Pam has one daughter, Becky, who graduated from college in 2002, and is getting married in 2004. Nannette, my next oldest child, is a nurse, and a very good one! She is married, and has two children, Leah, who was married in 2002 and Mark, who is in high school. Donna, another daughter is a model and has been for over 20 years.

BERNARDS TOWNSHIP RECREATION
ADULT OIL PAINTING CLASS
INSTRUCTOR: MS. SUZANNE BUCCERI

EXHIBITION OF STUDENT'S WORK

ARTIST	PAINTING TITLE
AGNES GORDON	Girl by Window Dana's Clown
EDITH HOGAN	Spring is Coming Darkness Falls
MYRTICE RYAN	Owl's Head Road, Owl's Head, Maine Piedras Blancas Lighthouse
MYRTILLA DONNER	Boats at Dockside Andrew
LORNA BUNTE	Summer Bouquet Pleasant Valley Park
MILDRED POOLE	Cape Cod Scene French Country Scene
ROBERT KENNEDY	Coppergate Farm Boys in a Pasture from Winslow Homer
RUTH WAURICH	Autumn in Vermont
EMILY GAWLEK	The Farm House Old Mill on Route 202
ESTELLE LUBIN	Evergreen Winter Winter Scene

The class is sponsored by Bernards Township Recreation. No experience is
necessary. Ms. Bucceri provides professional instruction and guidance to beginners
and to those with some experience in Oil Painting. For more information,
contact Bernards Township Recreation at 204-3028.

One of Lorna's many paintings.

Our "Dinner Bridge Group" (With one of
Lorna's paintings in the background).

She also has her own Acupuncture business. My son, David, is an environmental engineer. He is married, and has a son almost one year old. David spent many years working in Alaska. He is now in northern California. Linda, our youngest child, is an occupation therapist at a veteran's hospital in Connecticut. She is very active in her church and in women's retreats. She is not married.

My children have varying degrees of faith in God. I pray for them every day, and want them to know that I have found that my relationship with God is the most important priority in my life, and if they see anything good in me, it is because of that close relationship with God.

My children and grandchildren (left to right: Linda, Nannette, David, Becky - granddaughter, Leah - granddaughter, Pam, and Donna.

More Grandchildren.

Julia & Logan
(Donna & Michel's children).

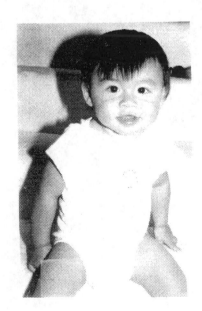

Michael
(David and Mei's son).

Mark
(Nannette & Mike's son)

1993
Twenty-Seventh
New Jersey
Senior Citizens
Annual Juried
Art Exhibition

Sponsored by
**The State of New Jersey
Division on Aging
Department of Community Affairs**

On exhibit at the
Monmouth County Library
125 Symmes Drive, Manalapan, NJ

September 14-29, 1993

**Monday through Thursday - 9 a.m.-9 p.m.
Friday & Saturday - 9 a.m.-5 p.m.
Sunday - 1-5 p.m.**

The exhibit features more than 170 winning entries from contests held in each of the State's twenty-one counties, sponsored by the County Offices on Aging. The state event is sponsored by the New Jersey Division on Aging, Department of Community Affairs.

This annual event has been held since 1967 and provides an opportunity for hundreds of senior citizens throughout New Jersey to display their skills and creativity by competing in a statewide contest.

SOMERSET COUNTY

† 138. Bunte, Lorna   Mountain Vista
    mixed-media - non-professional   2nd Place
139. France, Jeane   Untitled
    sculpture - professional
140. Higgins, Tomi   Blue Bell - Duke Island Park
    watercolor - non-professional
141. McNally, Ken   Gothic Aurora
    oil - non-professional
142. Nielsen, Jeane   Pink Polly Nose
    watercolor - professional
† 143. Pearson, Charles   Rat's Eye View of the Terminator
    photography - non-professional   Honorable Mention

Another of Lorna's paintings.

93

Condolences

To the family of Lorna Bunte who passed away this past week. Let us pray that she and all the recently deceased of our parish find the fulfillment of their faith in the loving presence of the Lord; and that their families will find strength and consolation in Jesus, and comfort and support from their friends.

Notice in the church news letter.

†

In Loving Memory of

LORNA E. BUNTE
Entered Into Eternal Rest
February 24, 1994

The Lord is my Shepherd; I shall not want. In verdant pastures He gives me repose; Before restful waters He leads me; He refreshes my soul. He guides me in right paths for His name's sake. Even though I walk in the dark valley I fear no evil; for you are at my side, with your rod and your staff that give me courage. You spread a table for me in the sight of my foes; you anoint my head with oil; my cup overflows. Only goodness and kindness follow me all the days of my life; And I shall dwell in the house of the Lord for years to come.

———

PAUL IPPOLITO
BERKELEY MEMORIAL
Berkeley Heights

Lorma & I in front of Marriage Encounter billboard in Lourdes.

On the way to Lourdes with Marriage Encounter Group (On
747 - I am in top photo, and Lorna in bottom.

Part of our group at Grotto where the Virgin Mary appeared.

Mass at underground church at Lourdes.

Close up of Grotto.

On train from Lourdes to Rome (Lorna on right).

We were this close to Pope John Paul II at general audience in Rome.

TRIP TO THE HOLY LAND

March 29 - April 13, 1982

Detail Agenda for Trip to Rome, and the Holy Land

Day 1—Monday, March 29 —Early evening departure on KLM from JFK to Rome.

Day 2—Tuesday, March 30— Arrive in Rome early afternoon. Check into Beverly
    Hills Hotel. Mass in the hotel.

Day 3—Wednesday, March 31— All morning: outdoor audience w/Pope John Paul II
    We see and touch him. Lunch at the Sardinian rest. Il Marlo.
    All afternoon bus tour: St. Peter in Chains (Michelangelo's Moses
    there); the Coliseum; the Pantheon; view the Forum, the Piazza Venezi
    the Vittorio Emanuel Monument; the Fountain of Trevi; the Jesuit
    Church of the Gesu with St. Ignatius' tomb.

Day 4—Thursday, April 1—All morning visit to the Vatican Museum, including
    the Sistine Chapel. Lunch at Armando's on the way to the airport.
    4 p.m. flight to Amman, Jordan, via Royal Jordanian Airlines.
    Arrive at Amman and check in at Marriott Hotel. Eat second dinner!

Day 5—Friday, April 2— By bus to Israel border. Wait our turn in the heat.
    Pick up our Israel bus and Anton, our Arab Catholic guide. Jericho
    for lunch. See the Mt. of Temptation, the Tel, Elisha's brook.
    Climb to Bethany and have Mass at Martha, Mary and Lazarus' Church.
    Brief stop at Italian Sisters in Bethany. Proceed to Jerusalem and
    St. George Hotel in East Jerusalem (the West Bank).

Day 6—Saturday, April 3—To the Shepherd's Field, the Herodion and to Beth-
    lehem for Mass. Lunch in Bethlehem.
    Back in Jerusalem, a complete tour of the Church of the Holy Sepulchr
    After dinner: to the YMCA for a folklore evening.

Day 7—Palm Sunday, April 4—To Ein Karem and the Visitation Church for Mass.
    Brief stop at the Church of St. John the Baptist. Visit the Kennedy
    Memorial in the Jerusalem Hills. Tour the Model of Jerusalem at
    the time of Jesus in the Holyland Hotel.
    After lunch, participate in the Palm Sunday procession, ending at
    St. Anne's with Benediction. Walk back to hotel for dinner.
    Slide show and lecture on the Shroud of Turin at Anglican Center.

Day 8—Monday, April 5—At 8 a.m., we leave for the Galilee via the Jordan
    Valley. Anton proudly shows us how the area is blossoming. We stop
    at Bet Alpha kibbutz to see the mosaics. On to Tel Megiddo (Arma-
    geddon in the Bible) and a walk through its tunnel, built in 8th
    century B.C.
    Lunch at Nazareth and Mass at the Basilica of the Annunciation.
    A brief look at Cana (Kfar Kenna) and on to Tiberias and our hotel.

Day 9—Tuesday, April 6—To the Mt. of the Beatitudes for Mass. On to
    Primacy Church, Capharnum, followed by boat ride to Tiberias.
    Lunch at the new Thermal Baths. Balance of day free.

Day 10—Wednesday, April 7— Leaving the Galilee, renew our baptismal promises
    by the Jordan, and go to Mt. Tabor for Mass. Go up in taxis, as buses
    cannot make the turns. Mass in the Moses Chapel, where some Colombian
    charismatics join us. They only speak Spanish but we communicate fin
    To Haifa, Akka, Caesarea and to Tel Aviv for our overnight.
    Seder in Marina Hotel.

Day 11—Holy Thursday, April 8—To Jerusalem, symbolically walking a few steps
    To the Mt. of Olives and: Mt. of Ascension, Pater Noster, Dominus
    flevit and Gethsemani Churches. Over to St. Peter in Gallicantu,
    where St. Peter denied Christ and Jesus spent his last night on earth
    to the Upper Room and back to the hotel.
    After lunch, back to the Mt. of Olives to the Polish Sisters for Mass
    with them and the children.
    After dinner, attend the Holy Hour in Gethsemani.

Day 12—Good Friday, April 9— By taxi to St. Stephen's Gate, and then
    on foot to St. Anne's Church of Crusader fame and to the Pool
    of Bethesda alongside. Then the Church of the Flagellation,
    the Place of Pilate's Judgment, and the Lithostrotes (in Ecce
    Homo Convent) the original courtyard of the Antonia fortress.
    The Stations of the Cross along the Via Dolorosa.
    Taxi from the Jaffa Gate back to the hotel for lunch.
    Afternoon free for visiting St. Anne's, Garden Tomb, etc.
    At 6 p.m. our own mass of the pre-sanctified at the Petite
    Chapelle of the White Sisters on Nablus Road.

Day 13—Holy Saturday, April 10—By bus to Masada. Detour to see the salt
    chimney cave at Sdom (old Sodom). Then the Masada experience
    and lunch there afterwards. We ride to En Gedi for a dip in
    the Dead Sea. Our last stop is at Qumran before returning in
    late afternoon to Jerusalem.
    At 6:30 p.m. our mass again at the White Sisters.

Day 14—Easter Sunday, April 11— Our Mass at 7 a.m. at the XI Station
    on Calvary in the Holy Sepulchre Church, returning to hotel
    for breakfast. Visits to other shrines in the Old City.
    The 1 o'clock showing of the Jerusalem slide show at the
    Citadel, followed by lunch at Notre Dame de Jerusalem.
    Afterwards, a walk through West Jerusalem to see the King
    David Hotel and a nearby art colony.

Day 15—Easter Monday, April 12— By bus to the Dung Gate and into the
    Old City to see the Temple Mount excavations and the Western
    Wall. Then by bus to the Shrine of the Book for the Dead Sea
    Scrolls exhibit and for a guided tour of highlights of the
    Israeli Museum. Return to the Jaffa Gate and walk to the
    Maronite Chapel for our own Mass.
    Lunch at the hotel and a free afternoon for revisiting holy
    places and for shopping.
    At 6 p.m. a short prayer meeting, followed by sharing of trip
    impressions and reflections. The Bunny Award. Joyful songs of
    experience and reminiscence.
    After dinner, the mass of the following day.

Day 16—Tuesday, April 13— Early departure for Ben Gurion Airport
    to enplane for New York. Late afternoon arrival at Kennedy,
    after changing planes in Amsterdam.

Father Joe reading the Scripture about the Garden of Gethsemane.

Close-up of Father Joe Neville during Mass.

Father Joe saying Mass for our group on Easter Sunday
morning in the Church of the Holy Sepulchr.

Part of our group (and others) coming out of the Church of the Holy Sepulchr on Good Friday.

THE JERUSA

POS

1932
50
1982

Monday, April 12, 1982

Security men seize Allan Harry Goodman at the end of yesterday's shooting on the Temple Mount.
(Rahamim Israeli)

Many hurt as Moslem crowds seek revenge

Two killed as crazed gunman runs amok on Temple Mount

By ABRAHAM RABINOVICH
and ISRAEL AMRANI
Jerusalem Post Reporters

An apparently demented American immigrant in Israel army uniform shot his way onto the Temple Mount yesterday in an incident that resulted in the deaths of two Arabs and the wounding by gunshots of more than a dozen others.

Ghawanima, the northernmost gate in the western side of the Mount. Dressed in army uniform and carrying an American-made M-16 rifle, which is widely used in the Israel Defence Forces, Goodman shot and wounded the Wakf guard and the Arab policeman posted at the gate who tried to stop him. Walid Junedi, an Arab policeman posted at Bab en Nadhir, about 70 metres _____ Goodman running

A 21-year-old Arab, Saleh Dari of Issawiya village, said he was praying near the Foundation Stone around which the shrine is built, when he heard shooting above him. He looked up to see the man with the rifle shooting at him. He was hit in the shoulder and hospitalized at the Hospice Hospital.

Goodman apparently fired out through the main door of the Dome of the Rock until his two magazines

Local newspaper with description of riot after an Isreal soldier
killed two arabs in the Temple of the Mount

102

Our group at church where we took refuge from shooting at the Temple Mount.

Garden of Gethsemane.

SOUVENIR OF GETHSEMANE

Lorna & I at Mt of Olives.

Lorna coming out of Salt Cave at Sodom

The lowest spot on earth*, in the Dead Sea and Jericho area.

_____

* at ground level

Road we took to the top of Mt Tabor.

Church at the top of Mt Tabor
(Fr Joe said Mass there).

Gates to the village of Capharnaum. (Part of our group).

Capharnaum - Fr Joe reading the scripture of what happened there.

The group that went to the Holy Land with Lorna & me and Fr Joe.

I am cutting grass at house in Berkeley Heights, NJ.

I am digging out rocky soil so we can plant a rose garden in good soil. (At our Bridgewater home).

Some of the sports I was interested in.

I am sking on Mt Tom (Massachusetts).

Tennis

Union Carbide Bowling League
I am top row - center
From the facial expressions you wouldn't know that we won!

Swimming and snorkeling.

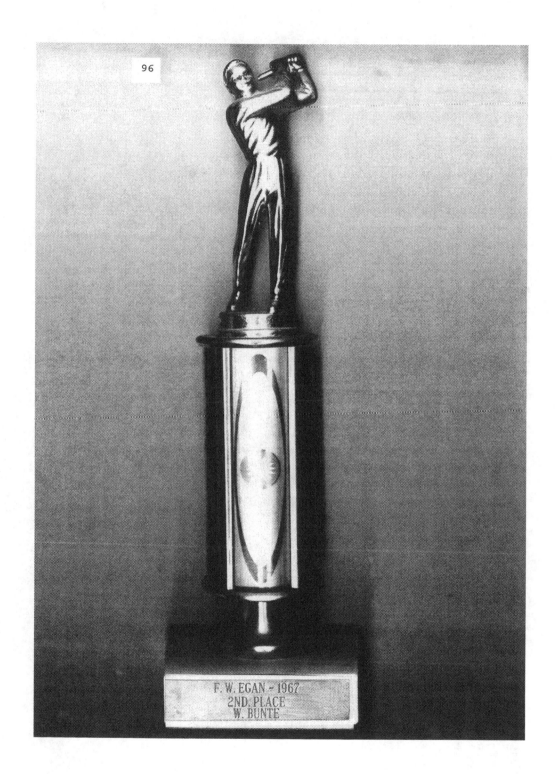

Pine Valley is a well-kept secret — if its members blab, they're out

Good golf, great food, but no welcome mat

By JUDY PEET

To be thrown out of Pine Valley, first you must find it.

There are no signs, but if you go to Clementon, a little scrub-pine suburb in southern Camden County, and ask around, the locals are quite helpful: Turn at Splashworld water park and follow the dusty, unmarked road along the railroad tracks.

At the end of the road, cross the tracks and, as Clementon Police Chief Robert Getz describes it, "you suddenly go from Kansas to Oz."

Like Oz, Pine Valley Borough is very green, and it is accessible by only one narrow road. A gatekeeper guards its portals, allowing entry to a select few. Inside is a land of enchantment where life is elegantly simple, where surprises are rarely ugly and where the snapper soup is fabulous.

Pine Valley is no fantasy. One square mile of prime real estate surrounded by a fence, it is a duly incorporated New Jersey municipality that has

the right of taxation, accepts state funding and is bound by state and federal constitutions.

Nobody seems to remember why Pine Valley incorporated in 1929, but its government now serves a single pur-

pose: keeper of the gate for Pine Val... Golf Club, which owns every inch ... land in Pine Valley Borough.

Pine Valley has no main street, ...

Pine Valley is administered from these bungalows ... the borough clerk's office at le... and the police departmen...

Photo by Tom ...

Please turn to Page 13

Continued from Page One

stores, no schools, no churches, no parks, no long-term parking, no crime, no tax delinquents, no municipal debt, no welfare. What it has is 18 holes of golf, 19 houses and a basic rule: If you want to own a home in Pine Valley, you have to join the club.

But you can't join the club if you are a woman.

Pine Valley, pop. 20, has no women homeowners, no women police officers, no women elected officials and no women full-time borough employees.

And Pine Valley has no intention of changing.

Not everyone favors this arrangement. Pine Valley is "the kind of Arab emirate-like situation that makes New Jersey government the butt of jokes," says former Assembly Speaker Alan Karcher.

The only reason that I was able to play golf at Pine Valley, was that my boss at Egan Machinery was a member and invited me. It was a very difficult course (I was very lucky to have 115 for 18 holes!)).

Photo by Steve Andrascik

Part of Pine Valley's golf course. Legend has it that President Bush once was denied a round there.

I am next to a very old RR engine.
Skagway, Alaska

Lorna in front of large glacier - Alaska.

Photo out the window of small airplane (4 seater) - near Mt Mc Kinley.

Close-up of large glacier - Alaska.

Photo of Mt Mc Kinley from airplane.

MY BUSINESS TRIPS (FOR EGAN MACHINERY),
WITH LORNA, TO EUROPE AND JAPAN.

Lorna in front of 10 Downing St in London, England.

Lorna & I in Copenhagon, Denmark

I am in Imatra, Finland (Russia is about one mile behind me).

Amsterdam, Holland
We were there but no picture.

Eiffel Tower - Paris.

Les Invalde, Paris, France

Japanese Temple - Tokyo

I am with Saburo (Engineer with our licensee and my guide while in Japan).

I am with Lorna in downtown Tokyo

Lorna in Kyoto

Lorna & I at restaurant with officials from licensee (and Ghisha).

享保の昔から培ちかわれた
日本の味　〈紙なべ料理〉

遠く江戸の昔から人々に好まれ親しまれて
きた　紙なべ料理。この日本独特な味は永
い伝統の中に守られてきた手漉き和紙の生
みだす生の味覚です。

五十種類の野菜と十種類の魚を一つなべで
──緑黄野菜等の豊富な香りと栄養も新鮮
な魚の風味も、個々の味覚がそこなわれず
に、あなたの舌にのり美食を楽しませてく
れます。

紙なべ料理のダイゴ味は《ワンダフルペー
パーパン》といって多数の外人客から親し
まれています。

Menu in Japanese restaurant.

熊田神宮　　　撮影 1968. 4. 12　　　名古屋市内遊覧記念

Lorna (back row - middle) on guided tour while I was working.

Part of Egan extrusion coating line - made in Japan.

120

I am with men from the licensee that I worked with.

Mt. Fuji

Kinkakuii Temple in Kyoto

Our trip to Oberammergau (Germany) to see the famous "Passion Play". (See next page).

350 Jahre Passionsspiele Oberammergau Jubiläums spiele 1984

Foreword

In the year 1633 when Oberammergau was in the grip of the black plaque, the inhabitants took an oath that they would stage a performance of the bitter suffering of Jesus Christ every ten years. For the first time in 1634 the inhabitants of Oberammergau fulfilled their oath, thus the village in the Ammer-valley will celebrate in 1984 the 350th anniversary of its "Passion Play".

For hundreds of years, in spite of dangers and threats, Oberammergau truly kept the solemn promise, a sign of loyalty and tradition.

With inner conviction the amateur actors are about to represent again the life and sufferings of Our Lord. Pilgrims from all over the world will be fascinated by the play, a testimony of religious faith.

Oberammergau, famous all over the world for being rooted to the soil, will demonstrate again that the play is still as valid as 350 years ago and has become an outstanding cultural event of our country.

Although text and music have been adapted to our present time, the amateur performers' original conception of tradition and the promised oath remained.

Passion Play. All actors are local towns people.

Heidelberg, Germany was a beautiful city
(especially if you like good beer!)

Diocese of Trenton
Family Life Bureau
presents this scroll to

Mr. and Mrs. William Bunte

on their

Twenty-fifth Wedding Anniversary

May almighty God bless you by the Word of His mouth, and unite your hearts in the enduring bond of pure love. May the Lord grant you fullness of years, so that you may reap the harvest of a good life, and, after you have served Him with loyalty in His kingdom on earth, may He take you up into His eternal dominions in heaven. Amen.

St. Mary's Cathedral
Catholic Family Day

Bishop of Trenton

Chapter 7

U.S. Navy Reunions

Fifty years after I was discharged from the Navy, I wondered if there had been any reunions Of the U.S.S. Mona Island. I called a reunion service, and they said that there had not been any reunions for our ship. They asked if I would like to start one. I decided to try to get one started. My wife, Jean, and I drove to the Navy department in Washington DC and we were able to obtain a microfilm showing the roster of the Mona Island as of 1945. (There were just names, no addresses.) On the Internet there is a Web Page that shows the names and addresses of almost everyone in the US. Some names had 2 or 3 different people with the same first, middle, and last name, but some had hundreds! We decided to send a postcard to names that had five or less different locations. It took several months, but we finally got thru all the names on the microfilm. We located 128 shipmates. Many were too sick to come to a reunion, but there were 35 shipmates plus 25 wives at this first reunion. It was held at a hotel in Williamsburg, Virginia for three days. We had a hospitality suite where we met. I would say a prayer at our first meeting of the reunion. (mostly for the shipmates who had died and those who were too sick to come). We spent a lot of time sharing stories (mostly funny) about various happenings on the ship. For example, the First Lieutenant was making "White Glove Inspections" while we were very busy repairing ships and trying to repel enemy air attacks. Someone put a rat trap on a high shelf where you couldn't see it. The First Lieutenant came to dinner that evening with two broken fingers all bandaged up. We gave him a "make believe" Purple Heart. We never had a "White Glove Inspection" again while we were at Okinawa! Also, no one was allowed to have a dog on the ship. Although none of the officers ever saw or knew that a dog was on board, one of the crew members reported at this meeting that there was a pet dog on the ship all during the war! The crew kept it hidden during all the inspections and all the other times that officers were around...

On the second day of the reunion, we would hire a bus, and go sightseeing in the local area and usually go to the local Navy base and tour one or more of the large Navy ships.

We would also have a "Dress Up" dinner at a local restaurant on the second evening of the reunion. We would give out prizes for the best story (as noted above), the couple who came the longest to the reunion, the oldest, etc. We would also get suggestions on where to have the next reunion.

We had a reunion once a year for five years. Besides the one in Williamsburg, they were held in South Charleston, Virginia, Virginia Beach, Va., Pensacola, Florida, and Portsmouth, Va. Each year the number of shipmates and their wives that came to the reunion was much less because of deaths and serious illness. The last reunion had only three shipmates plus their wives. Because of all the cost and preparations required, it was decided not to have any more reunions.

Men at first Mona Island reunion

GROUP PICTURE OF SHIPMATES AT REUNION

Front row (lft to rt): Paul Forney, Roscoe Mayhew, Jim McConahay, Bob Douglas, Charles Cambre, Rhett Lockliear, Gene Caste, Arthr Mack.

2nd row (lft to rt): Frank Malfa, Charkes Holloway, John Wrublevski, George Meder, Stanley Gop, Ed Dence, Joe Duffel.

3rd row (lft to restaurant) Ernest Jahn, Bill Waldron, Elmer Page, Ewing Threet, Ted Hejk, Robert Ashworth, Richard Slusarz.

Last row (lft to rt): Bill Bunte, Paul Hennecken, Bill Bratun, Clyde Long, Pete Vallet, Gordon Heal.

FIRST REUNION OF USS MONA ISLAND (ARG-9)
SUMMARY

The first reunion of the USS Mona Island (ARG-9) was held at the George Washington Inn in Williamsburg, Virginia from October 25, 1996 to October 27, 1996, although some came on October 24th and some left on October 28th. There was a total of 63 persons at the reunion (30 shipmates and 33 family members).

After the registration (5 to 6 PM) on Friday October 25th, there was a Wine and Cheese Party given by the hotel. This was a good occasion for the shipmates to get re-acquainted, as most of us had not seen each other in about 50 years.

At 8 PM on Friday, we met in a Hospitality Suite (which was ours for the weekend). The opening remarks for this meeting were given by Bill Bunte. After he welcomed everyone, he reviewed the schedule for the evening and the rest of the weekend. He also shared on how rewarding it had been for him in trying to organize this reunion, to talk to and read letters from many of the shipmates. He said it was also very sobering to hear from all the widows and the shipmates who were much too sick to come to the reunion. He said it really made him appreciate the gift of life, and after several near death experiences on the Mona Island and since that time, he thanked God for being alive and well enough to come to the reunion! Everyone at the reunion seemed to agree. At that point, we all prayed for all the deceased shipmates and their widows, and also for those shipmates too ill to come to the reunion.

We then had personal sharings about happenings aboard the ship by most of the shipmates. These sharings varied from the dramatic to humorous, but all were very good. Most of these sharings were based on the "Shipmates Comments", shown letter in this booklet.

After the sharings, there was time for fellowship, and time to examine ship photos and records that shipmates had brought to the reunion, as well as letters from widows and shipmates too sick to make the reunion. There was also a copy of the microfilm of the ships roster (from the National Archives in Washington DC), and computer printouts showing how shipmates were located.

Saturday morning and afternoon was spent on tours, shopping, and sightseeing, with the majority (43) taking the Norfolk Naval Base tour (9:30 AM to 3:30 PM). On this Naval Base tour, we went by bus with a guide, who described some of the points of interest on the way to Norfolk. At the Naval Base, a naval guide took over. First we toured the base by bus. Then we went to lunch at the base commissary (soup, salad, many entrees, drinks, dessert - all you could eat, for $2.89!). After lunch, we went by bus to the destroyer - frigate area of the base. We then took an excellent walking (and climbing!) guided tour thru one of the frigates. (To get to the frigate, we had to walk across a destroyer. This destroyer was larger than a World War II cruiser!). The 1945 navy ships were nothing like the new navy ones, with all the computer and electronic controls, guided cruise missiles, rapid fire anti-aircraft guns (hundreds of rounds/sec.), and many other changes.

Saturday evening, we had a delicious Smorgasbord dinner, and the group pictures were taken. We also gave the following awards:

Best sharing	Rhett Lockliear
Come the longest distance (Orinda, California)	Joe Duffel
Longest married (56 years)	Gene (& Lois) Casti
Oldest (___years)	

After dinner, we met in the Hospitality Suite and discussed future reunions. With a ballot type vote by shipmates on future reunions, the following results were obtained:

1) 100% voted to have future reunions.
2) 87% voted to have the next reunion on the East coast.
3) The frequency of future reunions: once every 1 1/2 years (There was an equal number of votes for a reunion every 1 year, and for a reunion every 2 years.)

During registration on Friday and throughout the reunion, USS Mona Island hats (caps) were made available to shipmates for $10 each by Paul Forney.

Sunday (October 27th) was free time for all. Most shipmates left to return home Sunday, although a few stayed and left on Monday.

From comments and observation at the reunion, and letters since then, everyone thoroughly enjoyed themselves at the reunion.

MIDSHIPMEN REUNIONS

There were 23 classes at the Midshipmen School at Columbia University during World War II that went thru the four month's courses. I was in the 18th class.

All 23 classes now have a joint reunion once a year. Jean and I have gone to two of these reunions. One was in Milwaukee, Wisconsin, and the other one was Portsmouth, Virginia.

The photo(s) below shows the midshipmen from the 18th class who were at the Portsmouth, VA reunion.

MIDSHIPMEN-USNRMS
18th CLASS-3rd. CO.

Bob Whiteside   **Don Clark**   **Bill Bunte**

Dick Lee   **Tom Kinkade**   **Don Larcen**

How it began!

Chapter 8

Married Life

Second Marriage:

After Lorna died, I was not interested in dating anyone. After about two months, I went to Jury Duty in Somerville, NJ and was assigned to a trial. I became friendly with one of the other jurors on the same case. His name was Jim. He was also a widower. We went out for lunch together during the trial. During our discussion, he asked me if I would be interested in going to a dance given by a widow - widower group called "The Wows". It was sponsored by the Metuchen Archdiocese. He also said he would like me to meet his sister. I said that I didn't think so, but I would think about it... I think the Holy Spirit, and also my deceased wife, Lorna, (she knew his sister), were nudging me to go to the the dance, because all of sudden, I decided to go! When I arrived at the dance, Jim introduced me to Jean. As soon as we met, we realized that we knew each other. I had known her husband, Bill, very well. He was President of the Holy Name Society, and I was Vice President. My wife had known Jean at the same time. Some of our children had gone to Immaculate Conception grade school, and Immaculata High School together and knew each other. I had moved away from Somerville, so didn't even know that Jean's husband had died. I am sure that this was not a coincidence that I was at the same jury trial as Jean's brother, that we met each other, and that I agreed to go to this dance that Jean was at. We had a good time at the dance, and I asked her for a date. I remember it was May 2, 1994 when we went out to dinner. During dinner, Jean said she was at this same restaurant recently with her brother, Jim. They were celebrating his birthday. I said that was interesting in that my birthday is May 2nd!

About that time, I was scheduled to go to Florida for a week course in a new business "Factoring". (More on this under the Business section of this book). This course was very demanding. The classes were from 8am to 10pm (plus homework) for six full days, and then a five hour exam. It was all worthwhile, because I did pass the exam.!

When I returned to New Jersey, Jean and I started dating. On the third date, I asked Jean if she ever thought about re-marrying. She said "Never!". However, I didn't give up. We kept on dating, and after several months, I asked her to marry me, and she said "Yes". We took trips to California and Connecticut (separate bedrooms), so my five children could get to meet Jean and she could get to know them. My children thought it was too soon after their mother had died for me to remarry. A very good friend of mine, whom I respect, said that my remarrying so soon, is a sign that I believe in marriage. I certainly had not planned on getting married so soon, but I also had not planned on meeting and falling in love with someone like Jean!

Certificate of Marriage

Church of

Our Lady of the Mount

Warren, New Jersey

This is to Certify

That   William Bunte

and   Genevieve Cullinan

were lawfully   **Married**

on the   24th   day of   September   19 94

According to the Rite of the Roman Catholic Church

and in conformity with the laws of

the State of   New Jersey

Rev. Msgr. William Benwell   officiating,

in the presence of   David Bunte

and   Mary Tramontozzi   Witnesses,

as appears from the Marriage Register of this Church.

Dated   October 31, 1994

Msgr. William Benwell
Pastor

We were married on September 24, 1994 at Our Lady of the Mount church in Warren, NJ. Our reception was at the Chanticer Chateau - also in Warren. There were 65 guests at the reception. Everyone seemed to have a great time. We went to a time share I had in the Poconos (Pennsylvania) for a few days, and then flew to Bermuda for a week for our honeymoon. There was a very bad storm during our first night there, and all the electricity was shut off, so we had no lights. (We didn't seem to mind too much...). The rest of the week was clear weather and we enjoyed it very much. The food was also very good where we stayed. We did a lot of sightseeing, and shopping of course!

After our honeymoon, we moved into Jean's townhouse in Bound Brook, NJ while my townhouse in Basking Ridge was being painted on the inside. Since my townhouse was larger than Jean's, we had decided to live there. Jean would then rent her townhouse.

Since Jean and I have nine children between us (five are mine and and four are Jean's) we have been doing a lot of traveling trying to visit them as often as we can. (Three are in California, one in Wisconsin, and three in Connecticut, one in Texas, and one in New Jersey).

Jean has three sons and one daughter: Patrick is a funeral director, Bill has a PhD in neuroscience, Bob has a MBA in marketing and Mary has a degree in nursing. Jean also has 10 grandchildren.

Even though Jean has retired from Roche Labs, and I am semi-retired, we live busy lives. I was working part time at my new business "Factoring" and more recently at my consulting business. Jean has been volunteering at the Somerset Hospital, the Bridgewater Library, and the Baby Center in Basking Ridge. She also volunteers at the Visiting Nurses Asso. when they have their Rummage sale (She works there a total of about 45 days per year).

We also took several interesting trips. One was a cruise to the Caribbean. Another was a tour thru most of Italy. In Rome, we were able to go to one of the Pope's General Audiences and see him very close in his Pope-mobile. We have also made numerous trips all over the US visiting our children, grandchildren, and various relatives.

Since I do not have a pension, and we live in one of the highest cost of living areas in the USA, it is difficult to do all this visiting with our limited income. However, we feel it is very important, for good family relations, to do as much as possible.

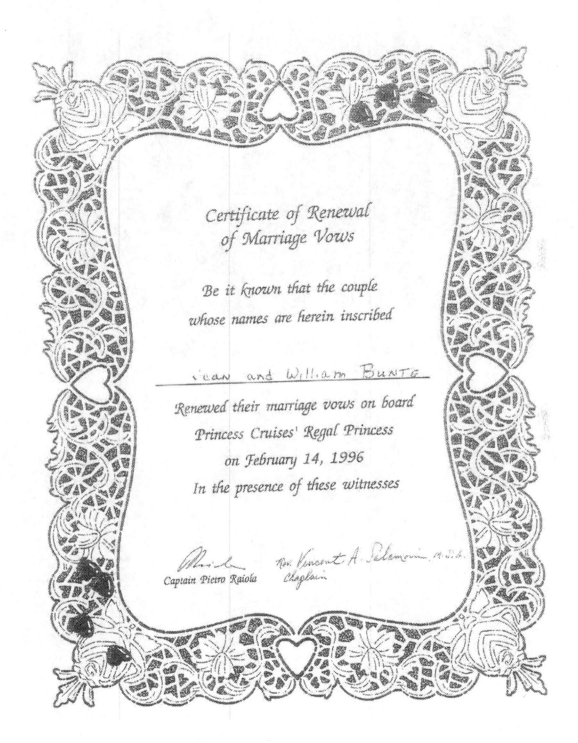

Certificate of Renewal
of Marriage Vows

Be it known that the couple
whose names are herein inscribed

Jean and William Bunte

Renewed their marriage vows on board
Princess Cruises' Regal Princess
on February 14, 1996
In the presence of these witnesses

Captain Pietro Raiola

Rev. Vincent A. Salamonie, M.S.C.
Chaplain

Renewing our Marriage Vows.

Jean and I with My brother Pat, and sisters Nanette and Helen during visit at San Antonio, Texas.

YOU ARE INVITED

"The Top-of-The-Hill" GANG"
(men Seventy and over)

To meet the Thursdays of Lent
starting Thursday, March 13.

From 8:30 AM to 10:00 AM
in Room 114 in the Parish Center.
(lower level of the church)

PURPOSE: Spiritual Reflection and Discussion
and Socializing

Deacon Jim Bell

These Meetings are held once/month
at St James RC church in Basking
Ridge, NJ. We have had some great
discussions. Some of us call our
group the "Over the hill gang!".

My Rice University (Class of 1946) 50th Reunion. Jean & I are in the photo (Somewhere!).

Bill Davis & his wife at 50th reunion of our class at Rice University. Bill was my best friend at Rice. (He and his wife have both died).

EDUCATIONAL DATA

Rice University - B.S. Ch. E. 1944
Rutgers University - Statistical Quality Control-Completed evening course (1955)
Dale Carnegie - Effective Speaking and Human Relations - Completed evening course (1964)
Alexander Hamilton Institute - Modern Business - Course three-quarters completed

6/1/46 to 6/1/50	Union Carbide Corp. Plastics Division), Bound Brook, N.J. Shift Foreman - Works Laboratory and Thermoplastic Inspection Direct the activities of 18 shift inspectors, testers, color matchers, color formulators, extrusion and injection molding operators in the testing and inspection of vinyl and polyethylene raw materials, intermediates, and finished products.
6/1/50 to 9/1/52	Union Carbide Corp. Plastics Division), Bound Brook, N.J. Chemical Engineer - Product Specialist Responsible for the control of quality of vinyl and polyethylene products, including film, rigid and non-rigid sheeting and planished sheets. Investigate complaints on products, including visits to customer plants to aid in solving their problems and suggest remedial action; develop special tests, and generally promote improved quality in these products.
9/1/52 to 9/1/55	Union Carbide Corp. Plastics Division), Bound Brook, N.J. Quality Control Supervisor Direct and coordinate the activities of four shift foremen, 66 wage testers, inspectors, color matchers, color formulators, extrusion and molding operators, three salary technicians, and two secretaries. Responsible for the operation and maintenance of the physical testing laboratory and pilot plant for vinyl and polyethylene raw materials, intermediates, and finished products. The laboratory testing equipment includes melt index flow testers, dielectric and power factor "Q" meters, tensile, brittleness, and tear testers, glossmeters, spectrophotometer, etc. The pilot plant equipment included extruders, injection molding machines, bamburies, two roll mills, and a four roll calendar.

Chapter 9

BUSINESS LIFE

Note:

A description of each job is shown on the opposite page for each business and was actually a reprint of my Resume of that job.

Chapter 9(a)

When I was discharged from the Navy in 1946, I started looking for a job, as did millions of other GI's! After applying for several jobs, I had two job offers. One was Pfizer Pharmaceutical and the other was Union Carbide (The old Bakelite Company). The pay rate was about the same from each company ($400* per month) to start. The training period required working shifts. Pfizer required working all midnight to 8 AM shifts. Union Carbide was rotating shifts (midnight to 8 AM one week, 8 AM to 4 PM the next week, and 4 PM to midnight the next week, etc).

I accepted the Union Carbide offer because the shifts were better, and the plant was in New Jersey. Pfizer was in New York City. I had prayed that I would make the right decision, and I now believe that I made the right choice. (However, you wonder. I found out later that the man who offered me the job at Pfizer became the president of Pfizer!).

In the training program, the production operators that worked with me were not told that I was a trainee. I was just a regular worker as far as they know. This helped me in my next position (Quality Control). They would show me all the short cuts (like putting their foot on a scale to get the correct weight, etc. The Banbury operator chewed tobacco, and spit the juice into the Banbury batch he was mixing. This caused some rejections in the finished product. There were other similar items that I observed. When I was assigned to the Quality Control Department, I was able to correct many of these problems. When the workers found out that I was in Quality Control, they were very surprised to say the least!

While I was on shifts, I got to know the foremen on the 4 PM to midnight shift. After the shift was over, we would go to one of the single foremen's house, and play poker until breakfast. It was a lot of fun, and I made several long term friends. After I got on the permanent day shift, and got married, I stopped the poker games. (It didn't quite fit in with newlyweds!).

I only used my college caleulus once in my business career, and that was while I was in Quality Control at Union Carbide.

---

* (Equivalent to $750. Today).

144

9/1/55 to 4/1/58	Union Carbide Corp. Plastics Division), Bound Brook, N.J. Assistant Department Head - Rubber-Modified Polysyrene Production. Manage Rubber-Modified Polystyrene Production Department, including the activities of four shift foremen, four assistant foremen, one secretary, one clerk, 52 wage extrusion operators, reactor operators, blender operators, drum dryer operators, and dye mixers. Responsible for the operation, maintenance, and scheduling of the following equipment: special twin screw compounding extruder lines,
4/1/58 to 3/1/59	Union Carbide Corp. Plastics Division), Bound Brook, N.J. Assistant Department Head - Polystyrene Production Manage Continuous Bulk Polystyrene and Rubber-Modified Polystyrene Production Departments, including the activities of eight shift foremen, four assistant foremen, one secretary, one clerk, 103 wage polymerization, dicer, color dispersion operators, (plus those shown in Rubber-Modified Polystyrene below). Responsible for the operation, maintenance, and scheduling of the following equipment: autoclaves, compounding mills, fractionating columns, condensers, (plus those shown in Rubber-Modified Polystyrene below).

Normally all the chemicals that made up a plastic product, were entered into a 2000 lb blender and weighed (The blender was on a scale). In this particular batch, all the dry chemicals were weighed and were in the blender, and the blender was rotating. Then they started adding the liquid plasticizer. At some point, before all the plasticizer was added, someone accidently opened the discharge valve in the blender. This meant that the amount of each ingredient in tbelender, and the amount of each item in the discharge was constantly changing. Before all the plasticizer was added, the open discharge was discovered, and closed. Without going into the details, I was able correct the a material in the blender, and the product that had been discharged, using calulus. Fortunately, I had taught calulus to some of the sailors in my division in the Navy. (See chapter on "U.S. Navy").

I worked eight years at Union Carbide, and all except the first six months were in management. I became Quality Control Manager after taking a statistic course at Rutgers College (nights). This was in the Vinyl and Polyethylene Department. After about three years I went to the Polystyrene Department and became Assistant Department Head of the Rubber Modified Polystryene Department. This was a very tough material that could be molded into various non-breakable items.

This was a difficult product to make, with lots of problems. The operation was run 24 hours/ day, seven days /week. I was working 12 to 14 hours/day.

The other half of the department was the straight Polystryene production lines. This was operated the same number of hours/day and per week as the Rubber Modified. The Assistant Department Head, Art, had different problems, but he was also working 12-14 hours/day.

I made some suggestions that would have reduced our hours, but the department head came up with his solution (?). He put me in charge of both production departments! I held on for 13 months, but it was too much, and I wasn't seeing much of my family, so I left Union Carbide. I didn't have any trouble finding a new job.

When I left Union Carbide, I was making $7,500.* per year. At my new job (Print-A-Tube), I started at $12,000.** per year.

---

* Equivalent to $14,400/year today.

** Equivalent to $23,300/yr. today.

Chapter 9(b)

Print-A-Tube Company

On March 1, 1959 I started at Print-A-Tube Company as a Quality Control Manager, R & D Director, and Assistant Plant Manager. This was an interesting company. I didn't know it at the time, but it was sort of an in-between company that gave me the experperience I needed in the extrusion coating and flexographic field that I required for my next job (Egan Machinery).

This company operated on a seven day week and 24 hours/day with four production shifts. There was a production Foreman on each shift. If there was a production or quality problem that the Foreman could not solve, then he would call me. I spent many hours there nights and weekends.

At the time, there were not too many tests available to check the quality of the finished product, so I had to develop some new tests to prevent returns from our customers.

The owner of the company had his wife working as the receptionist for the the day shift. She was a very nice looking woman. One day a salesman cornered me and asked "Who should I ask about getting a date with the receptionist?" I said the President - she is his wife! "Oh" he said and left...

After I had been working at Print-A- Tube for about two and one half years, The president retired and sold the company to an English company called Lassitar Corp. A few months after that Lassitar sold it to Regal Paper Co. By that time I was Plant Manager. I would have stayed there longer, but I received a very nice offer from Egan Machinery in their Extrusion Coating Division, so I accepted it. It was also back close to where I lived. I had been driving one hour (each way) to work at Print-A-Tube. Egan was only 10 minutes from my home in Bridgewater.

3/1/59
to
2/8/61

Print-A-Tube Company°, Paterson, N.J.

Assistant Plant Manager, R & D Director, and Quality Control Manager

Assist the Plant Manager to manage the extrusion coating converting plant described above. Responsible for control of quality of the flexographic printing and extrusion coating of polyethylene, nylon, and polypropolyene on various films, foils, and papers. Develop testing and processing procedures; investigate customer complaints, including visits to their plants; reduce wastes; develop new extrusion coated combinations and applications.

2/8/61
to
8/1/61

Lassiter Division, Riegel Paper Corporation

Plant Manager (Paterson, N.J. Plant)

Manage extrusion coating converting plant. Plan, coordinate, and direct the activities of one Office Manager, one R & D, Quality Control, and Assistant Plant Manager, two secretaries, one bookkeeper, one production clerk, five foremen, 18 pressmen, extrusion coating operators, slitters, maintenance, and shipping personnel. Responsible for the operation, maintenance, and scheduling of two flexible packaging extrusion coating lines, three flexographic printing presses, and slitter-rewinders.

RESEARCH • METHODS • TESTING TECHNICAL & ENGINEERING

CHARLES A. SOUTHWICK, JR., Technical Editor ROBERT J. KELSEY, Engineering Editor

Standards for extrusion coatings

Methods now in use for checking and controlling such factors as bond strength, heat-seal strength, gauge and basis weight suggest an industry-wide approach to the problem.

By Benjamin Lechner[*] and William S. Bunte[**]

President

Extrusion coating of polyethylene onto various substrates (cellophane, foil, polyester, paper) is a young and dynamic industry which in the past 15 years has become an important segment of the flexible-packaging industry. This technique was first developed in about 1946 and has advanced to the point where its products represent approximately $70 million a year. Further projections to 1965 forecast a possible increase of 100% and, in some items, the increase could be even sharper.

Because of the youth of the industry, quality-control standards have not yet been developed industry wide. With other packaging products, testing instruments and techniques can be borrowed from allied processes. However, extrusion coating of polyethylene requires its own peculiar testing instruments and methods of procedure.

Many extrusion coatings are used for packaging applications which make critical demands upon the films, as for example in flexible vacuum packages and protective packages requiring long shelf life.

In addition to the ultimate package itself being critical, there are more and more exacting demands being made by advances in the speed and accuracy of packaging machinery. To illustrate, we point to a pouch-making machine which runs polyethylene-coated cellophane at a speed of approximately 100 ft. per minute. It is not at all unusual for several different types of machines to form and fill packages at the rate of 100 per minute, at the same time synchronizing the packaging cycle to the printed message on the film. Therefore, in order to cope with the critical demands of the package itself and to insure machinability of films on high-speed packaging equipment, it is of vital importance that extrusion-coated films be produced on a consistently high and uniform quality level.

Certain protective properties of extrusion-coated films are "built in" by the selection of the type of

[*]

[**]   r, Print-A-Tube Co., Lassiter Div., Riegel Paper Corp., Paterson, N.J.

Figure 1. *Bond strength of a polyethylene coating is measured by peeling off a 1-in. sample on a Scott tester, Model X-5.*

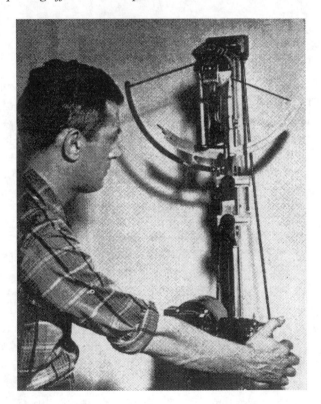

BUSINESS ASSOCIATIONS

TAPPI (Technical Association of the Pulp and Paper Industry) - Secretary (1966, 1967), and Vice-Chairman (1968, 1969) of the Extrusion Coating Committee.

PAPERS AND TALKS

"Standards for Extrusion Coatings" - Published in Modern Packaging (January 1961)

"Gravure's Contribution to Extrusion Lamination" - talk given at Gravure Technical Association Convention May 1966); paper published in GTA Bulletin (September 1966)

"New Techniques In Extrusion Coating Screw Designs" - talk given at TAPPI Paper-Plastics Convention (October 1967); paper published in TAPPI Journal (July 1968)

"Extrusion Coating Equipment For the Converting Industry" - paper to be published in Paper, Film, And Foil Converter (February 1969)

8/1/61 to 6/1/68	Frank W. Egan Company, Somerville, N.J. Sales Engineer Prepare detail quotations on custom-extrusion coating equipment (including the selection of the proper components and pricing); make formal sales presentations to customer; write Engineering Report (when order is obtained) to describe detail specifications on how the equipment is to be designed; act as coordinator between the customer and the Engineering Department while the line is in the design and manufacturing stage; assist the customer in the the start-up of the equipment; and act as the contact for subsequent problems, additions, new equipment, etc.
6/1/68 to Present	Frank W. Egan Company, Somerville, N.J. Product Sales Manager Manage the Extrusion Coating Sales Division including four Sales Engineers and one secretary. Develop marketing data on the extrusion coating industry; propose and work with Engineering and R&D Departments on new extrusion coating concepts and designs; write advertising copy; conduct monthly sales meetings; train Sales Engineers; assist in developing standard components and pricing; and participate in "Team Selling".

WILLIAM S. BUNTE
PAPER CONVERTING DIVISION

FRANK W. EGAN OF COMPANY
SOMERVILLE, NEW JERSEY
U. S. A.

Chapter 9(c)

EGAN MACHINERY COMPANY, INC.

I started out at Egan as a Sales Engineer in the Extrusion Coating Division. I soon found out that Egan was a great company to work for. The company gave a very liberal bonus to each employee in the company every year that I worked there (10 years). They also had a great system for the sales engineers. After he sold a job, then the sales engineer would work with the engineering dept in designing the equipment. After the equipment was built, then the sales engineer was responsible for assisting the customer in starting up the equipment. Once the equipment was running and a problem developed, the sales engineer works with Engineering to correct the problem. All of this experience would help the sales engineer in selling other jobs. The customer would also have some one to call if they had any questions on existing or future equipment. A complete Extrusion Coating line, including unwind, winder, printer, oven, and extruder, would cost between $200,000, and $ 2,000,000.

Egan was a leader in most of the equipment it sold. Many companies tried to buy it, but the President refused to sell. One day a company gave a very good offer of X millions. The president said Yes if he made it 2X millions. The man asked what the extra X millions was for. The President said it was the salary of his employees for the rest of their lives! The potential buyer went away shaking his head...

We were always trying to improve our equipment. One problem we had was the edge bead that formed when we coated a hot plastic on a film or paper in the extrusion coating process. Another person and I worked on this and found a solution. We were even able to obtain a patent, so that our competitors could not use use it.

We sold our equipment thru licensee's in other countries all over the world. So, besides the travel to companies in the US, we also traveled to other countries. When we had to fly to make these visits, Egan would let us fly first class. If we wanted to take our wives with us on one of these trips, the company would pay for two tourist class tickets. As I mentioned in the Marriage 1 section of this book, I was able to take Lorna to Japan and most of the countries in Europe, with Egan paying for the expenses.

One example of how the sales engineer works was an extrusion coating line that I sold to to a customer in Monteray, Mexico. I worked with Engineering in the design of the equipment to the customer's specifications. After the unit was manufactured, I went to Mexico for the start up. The person the company assigned to work with me could not speak English. I had taken Spanish in high school, but I hadn't used it since. We managed with hand signs, etc and my Spanish gradually came back, and the company man learned some English!

EGAN EXTRUSION COATING SPECIALISTS TALK AT WESTERN MICHIGAN UNIVERSITY

Bill Bunte

Dave Williams

<u>Bill Bunte</u>, our Manager of Extrusion Coating, and Dave Williams, extrusion coating sales engineer, gave a talk in January at Western Michigan University. The talk covered advances in extrusion coating equipment during the past 10 years.

Among the topics reviewed were web speeds up to 2500 fpm, increased extruder outputs and improved quality through computer-designed screws and dies, printing, coating, and priming in-line, as well as controls and equipment to handle lightweight and extensible webs. Co-extrusion, low temperature extrusion coating, air flotation and other recent developments were also discussed.

Winter 1967

EGAN MEN KEEP BUSY IN TAPPI

Jim Thornton

Bill Bunte

The first of the year, Jim Thornton, Sales Manager of our Paper Converting Machinery Division, became Chairman of the Paper Synthetics Division of TAPPI (Technical Association of the Pulp and Paper Industry).

The TAPPI Division headed by Jim, in addition to sponsoring the Annual TAPPI Paper Plastics Conference, supervises the activities of five committees: Extrusion Coating, Wet Strength and Inter-fiber Bonding, Plastics, Plastic Laminates, and Synthetic Fibers. Bob Sturken, our Vice-President and Treasurer, served as Chairman of this same TAPPI Division from 1958 through 1959.

Bill Bunte, our sales engineer for extrusion coating, is also active in the association's affairs. At the September meeting of the TAPPI Plastics-Paper Synthetics Conference in New York City, Bill was appointed Secretary of the Extrusion Coating Committee for a two-year period.

Bill tells us that his committee is presently writing up a test method for rating chill roll release, making a survey of extrusion coating problems and needs, and assisting in the preparation of a treatise on extrusion coating.

NFPA West Coast Meeting
October 18-21, 1970

Over 100 Members and guests attended the recent West Coast Meeting at Ojai, California. Photos provide a glimpse of some of the action.

G. Thomas Burrough (1), Dow Chemical Co., and Wm. S. Bunte (r), Egan Machinery Co., examine Tyvek sample held by George A. Scanlan, E.I. du Pont. The three were meeting speakers.

Automation and versatility show way to future

Since 1949, use of polyethylene in extrusion coating has grown rapidly: in 1969 it will require 360,000,000 pounds of polyethylene. Developments in the rapidly-growing field of extrusion coating and laminating were outlined by two speakers at Du Pont of Canada's Converting Laminating seminar in Kingston. Ont.

   <u>William S. Bunte</u>, sales manager, and Leonard C. Krimsky, sales engineer, both of the extrusion coating machinery division. <u>Frank W. Egan</u> & Co., Somerville, N.J., said that flexible packaging accounts for the largest number of extrusion coating lines. Of the 47 new extrusion coating lines sold in Canada and the United States during the last four years. 75% were for flexible packaging; 19% for coating on paper and 6% for coating onto paperboard.

NEWS
The Employees of Frank W. Egan & Co., Somerville, N.J.

WILLIAM S. BUNTE   **JAMES A. GIBBONS**

Two New Sales Engineers Appointed

Edward F. Egan, president of Frank W. Egan & Com-
ᵖ   has made two appointments to the sales engineering
sta   William S. Bunte and James A. Gibbons, both
experienced engineers. have recently joined the firm and
will specialize in tℎ   ɹe of extrusion-coating equipment.

Bunte, who lives in River Edge, N. J., is a graduate of Rice Institute and a former manager of Riegel Paper Corporation's Paterson plant. Gibbons is from Richardson, Texas, and has been employed since 1959 as a technical representative in the Texas region for Union Carbide Plastics Company of New York Prior to this he represented Union Carbide in the Mid-west for six years.

Bunte was associated for 12 years with Union Carbide Plastics Co. of Bound Brook, before joining Riegel Paper. He became assistant department head of polystyrene production while at Union Carbide.

Born in Kentucky, he lived most of his life in Texas before moving to New Jersey. Bunte is married to the former Lorna Pitz of New York. They have a son, David and three daughters, Pamela, Nannette, and Donna.

The Bunte family's most urgent project is to get their new home completed in Brian Drive,

---

HELP WANTED

> WANTED
> FOR SALES ENGINEERING
> POSITIONS
> Men with experience in
> Extrusion Coating
> Paper Converting
> Plastics Extrusion
> Please send resume and salary requirement to
>   Mr. W. C. Haulenbeck
>   Frank W. Egan & Company
>   South Adamsville Road
>   Somerville, New Jersey

238 Jefferson Avenue
River Edge, New Jersey
June 21, 1961

Mr. W. C. Haulenbeck
Frank W. Egan & Company
South Adamsville Road
Sommerville, New Jersey

Dear Walt

Enclosed is my resume with regard to the Sales Engineering position that we discussed on the telephone Also enclosed is a reprint of an article that appeared in the January 1961 issue of the MODERN PACKAGING magazine, which may be of some interest.

My current salary is the $14,000 per year. If there is any more information that you might want, I will be glad to discuss it with you in person.

Sincerely

William S. Bunte

Enclosures

How I came to work at Egan.

TAPPI Extrusion Coating Course Slated for October

Wednesday night, October 29

Panel Discussion: Maintenance of Extrusion Coating Plants.

Thursday a.m., October 30
The Extrusion Process
1. Components of the Extruder and their Functions: general description; functions of heaters, drives, and controls.
2. Extrusion Coating Profile Control: die design evolution; construction of dies and valves; current technology of die and valve design; screw design.

Polymer Fundamentals
1. Polymer Structure Related to Properties: molecular weight-melt flow; molecular weight distribution; density dependent properties of polyolefins——effect of branching.

Thursday p.m., October 30

Polymer Fundamentals–(cont.)
2. Polymer Structure Related to Processing:
Drawdown vs melt flow; neck-in vs melt flow and density; melt-temperature effects on profile and processing; pressure——effects on profile and processing; surging——effects on processing and product quality.

Adhesion in Extrusion Coating
3. Fundamentals of Adhesion: surface preparation and compatibility.
4. Polymer to Substrate Adhesion: oxidation and mechanical effects.
5. Priming for Adhesion: chemical adhesives; chemical coatings as primers; flame and electrostatic discharge priming.

Friday a.m., October 31

New Materials for Extrusion Coating
Properties of New Coating Polymers.
Processing of New Coating Polymers.

The following will provide instruction or serve on panels at the course:

W. S. Bunte, Frank W. Egan & Co., Somerville, N. J.
R. Cameron, Chemplex Co. Rolling Meadows, Ill.
J.P. Goslin, E. I. du Point de Nemours & Co., Inc., Wilmington, Del.
R. N. Henkel, U. S. Industrial Chemicals. Co., Tuscola, Ill.
E. J. Kaltenbacher, Monsanto Co., Texas City, Texas
R. E. Lowey, Jr., Gene Lowey Inc., Hamilton, Ohio
C. E. Roth, Gulf Plastics, Kansas City, Mo.
N. Reddeman, Morton Chemical Co., Woodstock, Ill.
K. Thompson, U. S. Plywood-Champion Papers Inc., Waynesville, N. C.
P. Yandow, St. Regis Paper Co., Pensacola, Fla.

It is expected that some registrants for the course will have attended the TAPPI Plastics-Paper Conference on preceding days at the Regency-Hyatt. Separate registration is required for the conference, whose program includes an extrusion coating technical session Wednesday morning, and a panel session Wednesday afternoon on "Trouble Shooting of Extrusion Coating Problems." The meeting of the TAPPI Extrusion Coating Committee, scheduled for Tuesday afternoon, October 28, is open without charge to all interested persons.

Vol. 52, No. 7 July 1969/Tappi

BILL BUNTE ANALYZES GROWTH OF EXTRUSION COATING INDUSTRY

Egan Sales Engineer <u>William S. Bunte</u> spoke at the 17th Annual Gravure Technical Association (GTA) Convention held in <u>New York last May</u>. In his talk, "Gravure's Contribution to Extrusion Lamination", he described the extrusion coating process, and the part played by Gravure in the growth of the extrusion coating industry.

Bill attributed the industry's phenomenal growth to technological advances contributed by converters' and users' development programs, by raw materials

Extrusion Coating Committee

The process of applying plastic materials to paper and paperboard substrates by means of extrusion coating.

C. C. G. GOODWIN, *Chairman*
W. S. BUNTE, *Vice-Chairman*
J. A. LOCK, *Secretary*

H. A. Arbit
J. E. Ayers
J. L. Bain, Jr.
D. L. Brebner
R. A. Cameron
B. A. Cooper
R. A. Costa
R. G. Cowan
L. E. DeGasperis
J. O. Dekle, Jr.
R. T. Delaney
G. G. Doubrava
R. A. Eidman
J. J. Forsythe
E. D. Graham
R. E. Greene
W. Haigb
A. F. Hardman, Jr.
M. Hecht
R. N. Henkel
J. A. Howells
A. R. Hurst
R. C. Ihde
E. J. Kaltenbacher
M. H. Kiefer
R. J. Kirchner
L. C. Krimsky
C. Kucher
R. G. Laumer
J. R. Lonsdorf

CONVERTING MACHINERY GROUP

Pete Russell, formerly Chief Engineer, has been named Converting Group Manager and will supervise the Converting Machinery Divisions which include Extrusion Coating, Paper Converting, and Printing. Harold Wrede has been named Product Manager of the Paper Converting Division and Alan Saunders Product Design Manager. Bill Bunte has been named Product Manager of the Extrusion Coating Division and Ray Peterson Product Design Manager. Fulton MacArthur has been named Product Manager of the Printing Division and Mike Schwetz Product Design Manager.

All of the personnel mentioned above are headquartered at Somerville, New Jersey.

In my position as Sales Engineer and Product Manager, I had to give a lot of talks and presentations. I had not done this in my previous jobs, and wasn't comfortable doing it. I decided to take a Dale Carnegie Public Speaking course. It was quite an experience. Besides the instruction on how to give a talk, and the experience of giving talks, there were other interesting additions. Usually, we would be assigned a topic to give a talk on at the next meeting. Sometime's the instructor would change the subject of the talk, to a new subject, as he was walking up to give the talk. This was to get us to think on our feet... They would also assign some students as "hecklers" to try to distract us as we gave our presentations... By the end of the course, I was actually looking forward to giving a talk!

The Board of Directors at Egan gradually changed over the years that I was there. After I was there 10 years, the Board actually voted to sell the company to an English firm. They did away with the bonus plan and other perks. Many of the employees left the company, including me. I decided to go into business for myself.

"EXTRUSION COATING & LAMINATING"

(This subject will be covered by two speakers)

MR. WILLIAM S. BUNTE
Somerville, New Jersey

Sales Manager, Extrusion Coating Machinery Division, Frank W. Egan & Company.

B. S. Chemical Engineering — Rice University. Vice Chairman, Extrusion Coating Committee of TAPPI.

**CONVERTER
LAMINATING
SEMINAR**

**May 25, 26, 27, 1969
the Holiday Inn
Kingston, Ontario**

The Technical Association of the Pulp and Paper Industry

Awards this
Certificate of Achievement to

W. S. Bunte

Recognizing the Completion of

Extrusion Coating Courses (Instructor)
taken under Tappi auspices

Lyle J. Gordon
PRESIDENT, TAPPI

John Lewis
CHAIRMAN
MANPOWER OPERATIONS COMMITTEE

GUSTAV LANGE, N.Y

New Techniques in Extrusion Coating Screw Designs

R. B. GREGORY and W. S. BUNTE

WE HAVE seen evidence of rapid technological advances in certain fields during the last few years. This paper describes an advanced technique in extrusion coating screw design with a computer.

Until recently, two principal methods were available to manufacturers of extrusion coating equipment to aid in selecting extruder screw design. One of these principal methods was based on past performance and the other on past empirical trials. Past performance data were kept for each feed screw design, listing results obtained from startups and joint trials with customers and resin suppliers. These data were then used to select a screw design for each new extrusion coating line.

The current coating extruder has been in evolution for a number of years, and the length/diameter ratio has changed from 16:1 to 20:1 to 24:1 and is now at 28:1. Screws with short metering sections have been replaced with the "50%" metering screw. Changes in extruder specifications for the coater are now in order. Barrel zone temperature control should include a cooling system of a high magnitude as far as heat removal is concerned. Water cooling meets this specification. Higher horsepower drives coupled with the proper "gear-in" speed are required for some of the new extrusion coating resins, and also for low-temperature as well as high-rate, high-temperature coatings. Finally, a radical departure is dictated in screw designs in order to upgrade current performance. The present extrusion coating quality standards are so exacting that extruder screw designs based on past performance and empirical trials are generally not satisfactory. The use of a computer and multistage screws are one approach in obtaining screw designs to meet the desired quality requirements. Results obtained with this approach are very encouraging.

Keywords: Extrusion coaters · Extruders · Screws · Design · Evaluation · Enthalpy · Computers

EXTRUSION COATING PROGRESS—PART VII

**Machinery
Developments
Jog Ahead**

Review of advancements in high speed extrusion coating focuses on tension controls, winding, drying systems and the design of extruder dies and screws

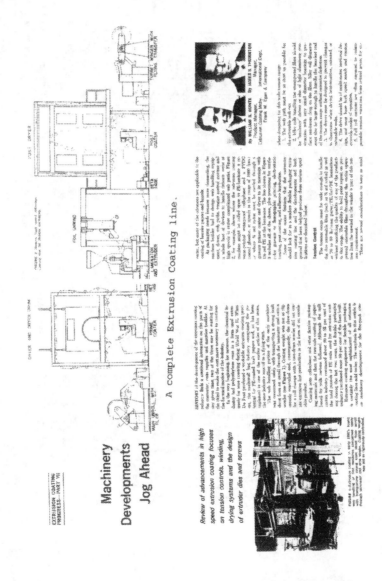

FIGURE 1–Extension coating in early 1950's found web handling of first machines concerned solely with transporting strong kraft sheet from unroll through laminator and onto winder. Coating weight was not as rigorously controlled.

A complete Extrusion Coating line.

HISTORY of the development of the extrusion coating industry finds a continual interaction on the parts of the converter, resin supplier and machine builder. At any given time, two of the three may be waiting for the third to make the next move necessary to continue the forward motion of the industry.

In the very beginning, for instance, the chemical industry had polyethylene resin in a form used extensively for wire covering during World War II. When Du Pont produced a workable extrusion coating process, the multiwall bag industry recognized the potential for PE-coated kraft papers and, as has been explained in one of the earlier articles of this series, the new industry was off to a flying start.

The web handling portion of the early machines was concerned solely with transporting a strong kraft sheet from an unroll through the laminator and onto a winder (see Figure 1). Coating weight was not as rigorously controlled and, consequently, the slow-down for a roll change with a two-drum winder did not create excessive lost production in the form of an unsaleable product

Coating onto cellophane and other flexible packaging materials and then the two-side coating of paperboard for milk cartons followed. Although the milk carton industry consumed about 80 to 85 per cent of the total pounds of PE resin used for extrusion coating during the last two years, the flexible packaging industry purchased same 80 per cent of the lines built.

Extrusion coating equipment for flexible packaging is certainly the most sophisticated of all extrusion coating lines sold today. The emphasis in this article is on machinery developments for the flex-pack converter, but many of the advances are applicable to the coating of heavier papers and boards.

As packaging needs became more demanding, the machine builder had to design web handling equipment, drives, web paths, tension control systems and a whole host of devices to handle delicate webs at high speed sin rather complicated web paths. Figure 2, for example, shows where the extrusion coating machine might be called upon to PE-laminate a reverse-printed waterproof cellophane and a PVDC coated glassine, at speeds in the range of 1000 fpm.: or where ¾ mil nylon must be carried through a gravure primer coater and dryer to its marriage with 1½ mil PE at the laminator. The line shown in Figure 3 includes all of the above, plus provisions for single-color gravure or flexographic printing, electrostatic treating, post coating, and adhesive lamination.

Some of the major features that the converter should look for in a modern flexible packaging extrusion coating line and the developments and background that have helped produce these various specifications are described below.

Tension Control

The tension range must be wide enough to handle the thin extensible films (such as ¾ mil nylon) as well as 70 to 80 lb/ream paper/PE/foil/PE laminations without sacrificing the quality of any of the products in this range. The ability to hold print repeat on pre-printed extensible films throughout the entire operation from the unwind to the winder is part of this tension requirement.

There are several considerations to keep in mind when designing for this wide tension range:
1. The web path must be as short as possible for the extensible web run.
2. Idler rolls handling the unsupported films should be "tendency" driven or else of light aluminum construction with very small diameter bearings to produce minimum drag on

the films. Idler roll diameter must also be large enough to handle the heaviest end of the tension range without excessive deflection.

3. The dryers must be designed to prevent changes in dimension when drying heat-sensitive, oriented, or extensible webs.
4. The drive should be of multi-motor sectional design, and must have both speed match and tension override modes of operation.
5. Pull roll sections are often required to isolate possible tension variations from critical areas; for ex

Computer Controlled Extruder Expands Converter's Capability

Brings Increased Production, Flexibility, And Quality

A CENTURY-OLD paper company is showing the youngsters new tricks in automated extrusion coating. Along 35 miles of the fast-flowing Fox River in northeastern Wisconsin lies the greatest concentration of paper mills in the world. Here, Thilmany Pulp & Paper Co. of Kaukauna just celebrated its 100th year of operation by starting up a new computer controlled extruder.

Called the CMR-200 microcomputer-control system and designed and built by Egan Machinery Co., Somerville, NJ, it features an infrared scanner that measures the moving film's thickness and signals a computer, which then converts the readings to degrees of temperature within thermally actuated die bolts. The individual adjusting bolts, mounted two inches apart, expand or contract as ordered to control the profile. Heating lengthens the bolt, reducing product gauge. Cooling the bolt has the opposite effect.

The coating thickness measuring system employs an infrared absorption gauge of advanced design. Several other types of measuring gauge can also be used with the die and control system.

In addition to controlling the die, the computer takes temperature, speed and other signals from the line, matches them with a programmed recipe, and changes con-

Thilmany's new Egan Extrusion Coater was designed from conception to make full use of computer control. It is equipped with an Egan CMR-2000/series 36 die profile control system and has programmable controllers for fully automatic unwind and rewind roll changes.

Computer Controlled Extruder Expands Converter's Capability

Brings Increased Production, Flexibility, And Quality

A CENTURY-OLD paper company is showing the youngsters new tricks in automated extrusion coating. Along 35 miles of the fast-flowing Fox River in northeastern Wisconsin lies the greatest concentration of paper mills in the world. Here, Thilmany Pulp & Paper Co. of Kaukauna just celebrated its 100th year of operation by starting up a new computer controlled extruder.

Called the CMR-200 micro-computer-control system and designed and built by Egan Machinery Co., Somerville, NJ, it features an infrared scanner that measures the moving film's thickness and signals a computer, which then converts the readings to degrees of temperature within thermally actuated die bolts. The individual adjusting bolts, mounted two inches apart, expand or contract as ordered to control the profile. Heating lengthens the bolt, reducing product gauge. Cooling the bolt has the opposite effect.

The coating thickness measuring system employs an infrared absorption gauge of advanced design. Several other types of measuring gauge can also be used with the die and control system.

In addition to controlling the die, the computer takes temperature, speed and other signals from the line, matches them with a programmed recipe, and changes con-

Thilmany's new Egan Extrusion Coater was designed from conception to make full use of computer control. It is equipped with an Egan CMR-2000/series 36 die profile control system and has programmable controllers for fully automatic unwind and rewind roll changes.

167

DU PONT OF CANADA LIMITED
FILMS DEPARTMENT
BOX 660 · MONTREAL 101 · CANADA · TELEPHONE 861-3881

30th May, 1969

Mr. W. S. Bunte,
Frank W. Egan & Co. Ltd.,
Somerville, N.J. 08876,
U.S.A.

Dear Bill,

The reviews are in on our seminar and it appears we have
a hit on our hands. We have been swamped with complimentary
remarks from both our customers and our own personnel.

A large share of the credit for this success must go to
you for your outstanding talk on extrusion coating and
laminating, and your participation in the panel discussion.
Everyone in attendance was greatly impressed. Please
accept my sincere thanks for your participation, and the
obvious effort that went into your presentation.

We have started typing the talks from the recording tapes
and in the very near future I will be sending you a rough
draft of your talk for editing prior to preparation of the
"Summary of Discussions".

Once again, Bill, many thanks for a great job.

Yours very truly,

DU PONT OF CANADA LIMITED

G. B. Prince
Sales Promotion Manager
Films Sales Division.

GBP:dh

FRANK W. EGAN CO.
RECEIVED
JUN 2 1969
FILE ....

SPECIALTY PAPER AND BOARD DIVISION
AMERICAN PAPER INSTITUTE, INC.

May 24, 1966

TO MEMBERS OF PLASTICS EXTRUSION COATERS GROUP:

MANUFACTURING SEMINAR

The Manufacturing Seminar sponsored by the Plastics Extrusion Coaters Group
held in Atlanta, Georgia, Wednesday, May 18th, was, indeed, an outstanding
success. The Extrusion Coaters Group's Chairman, Henry R. Eager, Jr.,
presided over an attendance of thirty-four persons in what proved to be
full-day affair. He expressed a few introductory remarks, particularly
attendees who had not been to Group meetings previously, as to some of
background, objectives, and, specifically, the whys and wherefores of the
session. Thereafter, he turned the meeting over to Paul L. Yandow, Superintendent of the Extrusion Coating Department, St. Regis Paper Company,
Pensacola, Florida, who acted as Chairman for the technical and manufacturing discussions which followed. Serving with the Chairman on a pane
were J. P. Goslin, of E. I. DuPont deNemours & Co., Inc., William S.
Bunte and James S. Thornton, of Frank W. Egan & Co., in their respective
fields.

The agenda followed the topical outline which was drawn up based on the
suggestions of members. The principal difficulty was the matter of tim
available to discuss such a tremendous listing of important topics.

By the meeting's own selection, most of the discussion was concentrated on
such items as control testing and coating uniformity; coating weight and
profile control; methods of weight checking; gauge or caliper variation
heat patterns and melt temperatures for light coatings; and pinhole con

At the end of a full day's program, it was the unanimous feeling of everyone that another Manufacturing Seminar session should be held, possibly
in the fall of 1966, and if a third one proves necessary, to schedule it
about six months thereafter. The matter of future Seminars will be re-
solved in due course by the Executive Committee of the Group and everyor
will be advised.

Enclosed is a list of all persons in attendance.

Sincerely,

George V. Johnson

HOT MELTS

William S. Bunte of Frank W. Egan & Co. spoke at length on recent developments associated with the extrusion coating of hot melts. Undoubtedly because of his background, much of his remarks were attuned to the machinery aspects. However, he did express a viewpoint that simplification in processing has opened the door quite wide for the coating of hot melts and their inevitable usage in certain packaging areas.

CHRISTMAS PARTY – 1972

Pictured below are candid shots taken at our annual Christmas party, held at the Far Hills Inn, on December 16. Over 400 people attended.

If you wish to have a copy of one of the pictures – call extension 322.

Pictorial Highlights of Company Picnic

Eganews, March, 1973

CHRISTMAS PARTY — 1972

Pictured below are candid shots taken at our annual Christmas party, held at the Far Hills Inn, on December 16. Over 400 people attended.

If you wish to have a copy of one of the pictures — call extension 322.

BUNTE AND WREDE TO PARTICIPATE IN TAPPI PLASTICS-PAPER CONFERENCE

We will be well represented at the 24th TAPPI Plastics-Paper Conference to be held in Atlanta October 27-29. W. S. Bunte, Product Sales Manager of Extrusion Coating Machinery, will be chairman of one session and serve as panelist on another. Bill and Harold F. Wrede, Sales Engineer for Extrusion Coating and Hot Melt Coating Machinery, will be instructors in a TAPPI sponsored short course on extrusion coating.

The technical session to be led by Bill covers extrusion coating and will take place Wednesday morning, October 29th. The panel on which he will be serving meets on the afternoon of the 29th to discuss "Trouble Shooting Process Variables in Extrusion Coating." Egan will have a suite at the Regency Hyatt House during the conference.

The short course, where Bill and Harold will be among ten of the country's leading experts serving as lecturers or panelists, will be held right after the Plastics-Paper Conference, October 29-31. It is the first such TAPPI course on extrusion coating. Subjects to be covered in depth are the extrusion process, new materials, polymer fundamentals, adhesion, and coating plant management.

Plastics Intelligence

Extrusion coating takes 360m.lb. PE in '69

Extrusion coating will account for 360 million lbs. of polyethylene in Canada this year.

This was forecast by <u>William Bunte</u>, sales manager, Extrusion Coating Machinery Division, Frank W. Egan & Co., Somerville, N.J., at a recent seminar held by Du Pont of Canada, Kingston, Ont.

Bunte added that of the 47 new extrusion coating lines sold in Canada and the US in the past four years, 75% were for flexible packaging, 19% for coating on paper and 6% for coating onto paperboard.

An important trend in extrusion coating is towards more automation, sophistication and versatility, improving profits by reducing waste and making more in-line operations.

Another development: low temperature extrusion of PE, melt temperatures of 400 to 500 degrees F. compared to the normal 600 to 620 degrees. This improves heat sealability and reduces odor problems.

Plastics Intelligence

BUNTE AND WREDE TO PARTICIPATE IN TAPPI PLASTICS-PAPER CONFERENCE

We will be well represented at the 24th TAPPI Plastics-Paper Conference to be held in Atlanta October 27-29. W. S. Bunte, Product Sales Manager of Extrusion Coating Machinery, will be chairman of one session and serve as panelist on another. Bill and Harold F. Wrede, Sales Engineer for Extrusion Coating and Hot Melt Coating Machinery, will be instructors in a TAPPI sponsored short course on extrusion coating.

The technical session to be led by Bill covers extrusion coating and will take place Wednesday morning, October 29th. The panel on which he will be serving meets on the afternoon of the 29th to discuss "Trouble Shooting Process Variables in Extrusion Coating." Egan will have a suite at the Regency Hyatt House during the conference.

The short course, where Bill and Harold will be among ten of the country's leading experts serving as lecturers or panelists, will be held right after the Plastics-Paper Conference, October 29-31. It is the first such TAPPI course on extrusion coating. Subjects to be covered in depth are the extrusion process, new materials, polymer fundamentals, adhesion, and coating plant management.

Extrusion coating takes 360m.lb. PE in '69

Extrusion coating will account for 360 million lbs. of polyethylene in Canada this year.

This was forecast by William Bunte, sales manager, Extrusion Coating Machinery Division, Frank W. Egan & Co., Somerville, N.J., at a recent seminar held by Du Pont of Canada, Kingston, Ont.

Bunte added that of the 47 new extrusion coating lines sold in Canada and the US in the past four years, 75% were for flexible packaging, 19% for coating on paper and 6% for coating onto paperboard.

An important trend in extrusion coating is towards more automation, sophistication and versatility, improving profits by reducing waste and making more in-line operations.

Another development: low temperature extrusion of PE, melt temperatures of 400 to 500 degrees F. compared to the normal 600 to 620 degrees. This improves heat sealability and reduces odor problems.

LETTERS PATENT

Patentee: Egan Machinery Company
South Somerville Road
Somerville, New Jersey
U. S. A.

Nationality: U. S. A.

Inventor: William Shute Bunte

Title of Invention: "Flexible film extrusion apparatus"

I hereby certify that the above-mentioned invention, having been declared patentable, has now been entered in the Register of Patents.

January 27, 1980

Director of the Patent Office

To All Whom It May Concern:

Be it known that WE, WILLIAM TRAIN BUNTE, a citizen of the United States of America, residing at Somerville, County of Somerset and State of New Jersey, HAROLD FRANZ WREDE, a citizen of the United States of America, residing at Brookside, County of Morris and State of New Jersey, have invented certain new and useful improvements in the

METHOD AND APPARATUS FOR CONTROLLING EXTRUDED FILM EDGES

of which the following is a specification

In a film extrusion process, one or more jets of heated gaseous fluid are directed against each side of the extruded film adjacent and inwardly of each edge of the film in closely spaced relation to the corresponding and of the extrusion orifice of an extrusion die, the jets preferably being formed by nozzles slidably mounted on deckle carriers that are adjustably mounted on the die.

My one and only patent.

United States Patent

Bunte et al.

[15] 3,694,132

[45] Sept. 26, 1972

[54] EXTRUSION DIE DECKLE MEANS

[72] Inventors: William S. Bunte, Somerville; Lino E. De Gasperis, Clinton, both of N.J.

[73] Assignee: Egan Machinery Company

[22] Filed: Jan. 21, 1971

[21] Appl. No.: 108,459

[52] U.S. Cl. 425/466
[51] Int. Cl. B29d 11/04
[58] Field of Search .... 18/12 DS, 13 F; 425/466

[56]   References Cited

UNITED STATES PATENTS

3,293,889	12/1966	Chiselko	18/12 DS
2,982,995	5/1961	Groleau	18/12 DS
3,018,515	1/1962	Sneddon	18/12 DS
3,107,191	10/1963	Brownold	18/12 DS X
3,238,563	3/1966	Hoffman	18/12 DS
3,443,277	5/1969	Frielingsdorf	18/12 DS
2,712,155	7/1955	Nelson	18/12 DS X
3,464,087	9/1969	Koch	18/12 DS

Primary Examiner—J. Spencer Overholser
Assistant Examiner—Ben D. Tobor
Attorney—F. J. Pisarra

[57]   ABSTRACT

An extrusion die having a discharge orifice in the form of a relatively long narrow slot and adapted to extrude a film or sheet of a flowable plastic material. The die is equipped with external deckle means adjustably positioned along the outer end of the discharge orifice and internal deckle means adjustably positioned along the inner end of the discharge orifice. The die and the external and internal deckle means are so constructed and arranged as to effectively regulate and control both the width and the thickness of a plastic film or sheet that is extruded from the die.

12 Claims, 14 Drawing Figures

The english version of my patent.

EGAN
LEESONA CORP

May 5, 1980

Mr. William S. Bunte
8 Brian Drive
Bridgewater, NJ 08807

Dear Bill:

Enclosed are copies of Japanese patents 984,680 and 991,905 recently issued.

Sincerely,

DAV/jet
enclosures

David A. Verner

A small portion of my patent.
(I decided that no one would
be interested in any more!),

A small portion of my patent. (I decided that no one would be interested in any more!),

DALE CARNEGIE COURSE
CLASS No. 33   PLAINFIELD N.J.

JANUARY, 1965

Giving a talk at class.

Giving a talk at class.

BUSINESS ASSOCIATIONS

TAPPI (Technical Association of the Pulp and Paper Industry) - Secretary (1966, 1967), and Vice-Chairman (1968, 1969) of the Extrusion Coating Committee.

PAPERS AND TALKS

"Standards For Extrusion Coatings" - Published in Modern Packaging (January 1961)

"Gravure's Contribution to Extrusion Lamination" - talk given at Gravure Technical Association Convention (May 1966); paper published in GTA Bulletin (September 1966)

"New Techniques in Extrusion Coating Screw Designs" - talk given at TAPPI Paper-Plastics Convention (October 1967); paper published in TAPPI Journal (July 1968)

"Extrusion Coating Equipment For The Converting Industry"
- paper to be published in Paper, Film, and Foil Converter (February 1969)

HOBBIES

Golf
Gardening
Camping
Reading

Chapter 9(d)

COLLEX

After I left Egan, I started looking for a business for myself. I looked into all kinds, including franchises. I finally finally found one that I thought I would like. It was an auto body repair that was franchised by a company called Collex. They would buy a auto body repair shop and then fix it up and sell it as a franchise. They took me to four different Collex shops so I could get an idea what they were like. I could talk with owners and ask any questions that I wanted. I could also look at their financial records. It was very clear that they were all very profitable ($100,000 to $250,000 per year).* When I said I was interested, they sent me to their school for three months* to learn about the business, including how to estimate a repair job. The repair shop they had in mind for me was in Kenilworth, NJ and was one of the largest in NJ. It would cost $100,000 to buy this franchise plus $1,000/month. I figured that I could pay off the $100,000 in six months to a year. So I decided to buy the business.

Once we started operating, I found out that you had to bribe the insurance adjusters in order to obtain an estimate from the insurance company, and 90 to 95 percent of all repairs came thru the insurance companies. I decided that I would not bribe the adjusters. When I refused to bribe, the adjusters stopped estimating. Most of the previous work came from one large insurance company. I made an appointment with one of the officers in this insurance company. We had lunch together. When I told him my problem, he said that he was hired to get rid of this problem. After we finished eating, he said that if we want any of his business in the future, we would have to bribe the adjusters, and send him a case of a certain brand of liquor for Christmas (in three weeks), and fix his Cadillac, that he just "totalled", at no charge - if we wanted any more of his business!

I then put the business up for sale, but couldn't get a buyer. With the $1,000./month franchise charge and no business coming in, I was forced to go out of business. I found out years later, from one of employees at my franchise, that the Mafia was very much involved in the auto body repair

---

* They told me everything I needed to know - except the most important (Bribing the adjusters)....

business. He also knows that the Mafia prevented me from getting a buyer. They wanted me to go bankrupt, so that they could buy it at a very low price, which they did, he said. I lost the $100,000 I had invested. (My life savings....).

I had always prayed that I would make the right decision before changing jobs, and I did before I bought the Collex Business. I have wondered why God let me go ahead and buy Collex.. As I write this book, I now believe that He was testing me - to see if I would put Him first, no matter what the cost...,

1973 - 1982   Automatic Industrial Machines, Inc.
Lodi, New Jersey
Position: President
Number of employees: 10 to 30.
Managed the manufacture and sales of material handling equipment.

Chapter 9(e)

Automatic Industrial Machine

After the fiasco at Collex, I decided to go back working for someone else.

I went to an employment agency and they had an opening for a president of a company that manufactured and sold conveyors. It was called Automatic Industrial Machines (AIM), and was in Lodi, NJ.

I made an appointment to meet with the owner. When I arrived, the president was tied up with his lawyer. While I was waiting, I went to the mens room. When I came out, the lawyer was there to take me to see the owner of the company. All he said was "Your fly is open!" How is that for first impressions? After the president reviewed my resume, he asked many questions. One was "Why did I leave the auto body repair business?" When I told him, he said "You are hired!" I then found out that the previous president was fired because he was caught stealing company funds. So being "honest" was evidently one of his main concerns.

When I started with the company, there were 30 employees. However, it was evident that they were not all needed and some were doing a poor job. By eliminating the latter, and installing a profit sharing plan for all employees (like the one we had at Egan Machinery), we eventually were able to have a higher quality product with more production, and only 10 employees.

During the recession in 1972 and 1973, the number of orders dropped so much that we had a serious cash-flow problem. I met with our accountant and he said that if we didn't receive $30,000 of new money in the next two weeks, we would have to go out of business. He said that because the company had a profit in both 1970 and 1971, it would be possible to obtain this $30,000. from the IRS. However, he said the quickest we could get this money would be five months... As I was driving away from his office I realized that God was the only one who could make this happen. So I prayed "Lord Jesus, please help me find a way to save our company. The employees need their jobs, but I can't do it by myself. I put my trust in you..." I then heard these words "Go to Holtsville"!. I didn't have any idea where Holtsville was, so I turned the car around and went back to the Accountant. He said that Holtsville is way out on Long Island, almost to the end. He said that it is an IRS restricted area, and only employees are allowed inside. There is also no listed phone number.

Part of AIM booth at Material Handling Trade Show in Chicago-
showing some of the tubular conveyors made by AIM.

I figured that God knew what he was talking about, so I got back in my car and started driving out the Long Island Expressway. After a very long drive I saw an exit "Holtsville" I took the exit, but I couldn't find any signs or even buildings. Finally I saw a very high wire fence. I followed the fence until I came to a gate house with an armed guard. I told the guard my problem, but he said that only employees could enter the IRS building. So I prayed again, and kept talking with the guard. After about 20 minutes, he called someone inside, and a few minutes later someone came out to get me and bring me to the person that was handling AIM's account. When I explained our problem, she said she would take care of it. Within two weeks we had our $30,000!

At AIM, we had 32 Sale Representives. They were all over the US, and also in Canada and Mexico. One of my duties was to visit them every few months to help them get orders from the leads that we would send to them, as well as leads that they would get on their own. We would also exhibit our equipment in two to four Material Handling trade shows per year. These shows were usually in the larger cities, such as Chicago, New York, and Los Angeles.

The owner of AIM had some serious problems with his other business, so he offered AIM to me at a very low price. At this point, AIM was doing very well, so I decided to buy it. It was a great small company. I had a company car, a salary of $50,000/yr, (equivalent to $109,000 at todays money value), plus a large bonus. The only problem, was that I was away from my family for a large percent of each month... At that time, I was involved with a Charismatic Prayer Group. One of the items that they emphasized was priorities in your life: God first, wife second, children third, business fourth, and everything else last. I knew that I had to change my priorities, so I prayed that I would make the right decision. Although it wasn't the best time, I decided to sell the company. It took several months, but I finally did get a buyer (and he got a good buy!).

I had been selling solar collectors, part time, while I was at AIM. I decided to go full time, and work out of my home office. I am glad that I made the decision to sell AIM, because I was able make up some of the time that I had been absent from my family.

Automatic Industrial Machines Inc.
115 Dell Glen Avenue
Lodi, New Jersey 07644
Phone: (201) 772-1100

December 11, 1974

Mr. William S. Bunte
Automatic Industrial Machines, Inc.
115 Dell Glen Avenue
Lodi, New Jersey 07644

Dear Bill:

Please be advised that Sanford R. Ross and the writer
discussed the salary remuneration which we agree to
increase as of December 1, 1974, to $30,000.00 per
year.

We have also agreed to design a bonus arrangement for
you which would take into consideration the sales volume
and profitability of the Company. Would you please assist
us in designing this arrangement so that, at our next
meeting in January, 1975 we can conclude such a bonus
arrangement.

I personally want to thank you for your efforts and
the timeless work you have performed to get A.I.M. organized in the manner that we have discussed at our
numerous meetings. Best wishes.

Kindest regards,

Irving B. Green

IBG;jcr

This $30,000 went up $50,000
in the next few years

182

AGRO—Technology Systems, Inc., Irv Green
421 SANTA ROSA DRIVE
Phone: (714) 325-7644   Cable: AGROTECK
PALM SPRINGS, CALIF. 92262

Mr. William Bunte   A.I.M.
115 Dell Glen Ave
Lodi New Jersey 07644

Dear Bill
I received the check & sent a
note to Mr. Jack Lynch to release the
A.I.M. stock to you.
I want to wish you
continued success with your
company & hopefully it will grow
into whatever you wish.
I trust to that you personally have
health, happiness in the future.
Best regards   Irv

BY: _____
JOHN F. LYNCH, JR.

CARPENTER, BENNETT & MORRISSEY

JAMES D. CARPENTER (1909-1975)

ELMER J. BENNETT   MICHAEL S. WATERS
THOMAS L. MORRISSEY   ANTHONY C. PANGALLO
ARTHUR N. LIZZA   JAMES D. GARDNER
WARREN LLOYD LEWIS   JOHN R. LYNCH, JR.
LAURENCE REICH   FRANCIS X. O'BRIEN
STANLEY WEISS   DONALD A. ROMANO
JOHN C. HEAVEY   ROBERT E. RUFFE
JOHN R. KEALE   FRANCIS X. DEE
EDWARD F. RYAN   RUDY A. COLEMAN
JEROME J. GRAHAM, JR.   EDWARD F. DAY, JR.
VIRGINIA D. PENTONY   DEAN A. WAY
JAMES J. CROWLEY, JR.   JEROME E. SHARFMAN
JOHN K. OWENS   JONVAS J. HOROWITZ
DAVID M. McCANN

SYLVESTER C. SMITH, JR. OF COUNSEL

LAW OFFICES
744 BROAD STREET
NEWARK, N.J. 07102

TELEPHONES
NEW JERSEY 622-7711
AREA CODE 201
NEW YORK 943-6520
AREA CODE 212

TELEX
120402

February 19, 1982

Mr. William S. Bunte
AUTOMATIC INDUSTRIAL MACHINES, INC.
115 Dell Glen Avenue
Lodi, New Jersey   07644

Re: Stock of AIM

Dear Mr. Bunte:

Pursuant to Irv Green's letter of February 16, 1982
(a copy of which I attach for your reference), I enclose the
balance of the stock of AIM held in our possession (Stock
Certificate No. 8 - 367.5 shares) issued in the name of
William S. Bunte. By copy of this letter, Mr. Green is
being advised of this transaction.

Very truly yours,

CARPENTER, BENNETT & MORRISSEY

BY: _____
JOHN F. LYNCH, JR.

/dms
Enc.
cc: Mr. Irving Green (w/enc.)

Purchase of A.I.M. from
owner (Irving Green).

183

I was invited by the Mayor of Lodi, NJ to a Republician Party meeting in Lodi in 1980. Ronald Regan was present at this meeting. (I took the above picture).

1983 - 1987   Natural Energy Sales & Consultants, Inc. Berkeley Heights, New Jersey
Position: President
Distributor and sales representative for solar heating, heat recovery, incinertion, and cogeneration equipment. Sales were more than doubled each year.

BIO-ENERGY SYSTEMS CO.
Solar & Heat Transfer Products

Product Line Overview

SOLAR ABSORBERS

Bulk Rolls or Modules (600 lin. ft. rolls or pre-assembled modules)
- Up to 4' x 80' pre-assembled absorbers
- Counterflow or grid pattern options
- Freeze tolerant
- Copper or plastic manifolds
- 6 U.S. patents--over 6,000,000 square feet in use
- Used in many forms of heat transfer applications

POOL HEATING SYSTEMS
SolaRoll™ and SunMat™
- Bonds to roof without penetrating fasteners
- Low profile, good aesthetic appearance
- No racks required

Chapter 9(f)

Natural Energy Sales & Consultants

During the oil shortage (1971 to 1976) I became interested in solar heating. I installed solar collectors on the roof of my house to heat some of the water coming from the water company. It worked so well, and saved enough on our gas bill, that I had it installed on the building where I worked (Automatic Industrial Machines} to help heat the plant and the hot water there. This was also a worthwhile savings.

I went to an energy trade show to learn more about solar heating, and saw a small exhibit with a very interesting design for the collector. It was made with a special black plastic that was resistant to sunlight. This material had been extruded to a flat sheet about 24 inches wide and with very small tubes (about 3/8 inch in diameter). These tubes were very close to each other and were part of the 24 inch wide sheet. This sheet would be glued to the house or plant roof and would be connected to "headers" at each end so cool water could enter at one end and heated water come out the other end. (A standard solar collector would be about 3 feet wide and 6 feet long in an enclosed metal framed box and with a glass top. Several would be required for each job, and they were very expensive.)

The inventor of this unusual collector was the only person in his booth. He answered all my questions, and then invited me to come and visit his plant near Kingston, NY. I went to the address he gave me, and found out that he was working out of his garage! He was also the only one in his company (Besi Corp*.). He asked me if I was interested in investing in his company. He said that he only needed 8 to 10 investors and each share was $4,000. I could see the potential for this company, but $4,000. was a lot of money for me. I said that I would let him know. I prayed that I would make the right decision (for about a week). I finally decided to buy one share.

I also became Besi Corp's* first Distributor. I called my company "Natural Energy Sales & Consultants Inc". This solar product (called "Solaroll" turned out to be very successful. I was able to sell installations to heat swimming pools (two Bahama Princess Hotels, a large hotel in

Bermuda, other large hotels in Cape May, NJ), and to heat Overlook Hospital's hot water and many others- both commercial and residential.) Another large application of Solaroll was the radiant heating of schools, and homes, where the plastic tubing is placed on the ground, and concrete is poured over the tubing and hot water circulated thru the tubing. One of my jobs was a new school in North Jersey, where the entire school was heated in this manner. Another was a 200 foot long driveway (with a turn-around circle) that was heated with radiant heat to eliminate snow plowing.

AGREEMENT BETWEEN WILLIAM S. BUNTE, AND BIO-ENERGY SYSTEMS, INC.

It being the intention of BESI to sell capital stock in the company to Mr. Bunte, at the terms stated below, the following agreement is entered into:

As the going rate for capital stock is $4000,00 per share, and BESI had previously quoted a lower figure to Mr. Bunte, the following terms are agreed upon:

BESI will sell one share of stock at $4000.00 per share, to be bought 3/9/78, and the others to be bought at a future date, not to exceed 6 weeks from the date of signing, unless agreed to by BESI.

One additional share will be priced at $4000.00 per share.

Mr. Bunte has the option of buying three additional shares at the total price of $10,000.00

If additional stock is desired by Mr. Bunte, it can be bought at the prevailing rate, at the option of the Board of Directors of BESI.

Mr. Bunte is not obligated to buy additional stock at any time.

Agreed to the 9th day of March, 1978 by   _____

William S. Bunte

_____

Michael F. Zinn, Pres. BESI
received $4000.00 date 3/9/78

AGREEMENT BETWEEN WILLIAM S. BUNTE AND
BIO-ENERGY SYSTEMS, INC.

It being the intention of BESI to sell capital stock in the company to Mr. Bunte,
at the terms stated below, the following agreement is entered into.

As the going rate for capital stock is $4000.00 per share, and BESI has
previously quoted a lower figure to Mr. Bunte, the following terms are
agreed upon:

BESI will sell one share of stock at $4000.00 per share, to be bought
3/9/78, and the other to be bought at a future date, not to exceed 2 weeks
from the date of signing, unless agreed to by BESI.

One additional share will be priced at $4000.00 per share.

Mr. Bunte has the option of buying the six additional shares at the total
price of $10,000.00

If additional stock is desired by Mr. Bunte, it can be bought at the prevailing
rate, at the option of the Board Of Directors of BESI.

Mr. Bunte is not obligated to buy additional stock at any time.

Agreed to the 9th day of March, 1978 by _____
                                         William S. Bunte

                                      _____
                                      Michael F. Zinn , Pres. BESI

received _____ date 3/9/78

Roof of house covered with Solaroll - to heat domestic hot water (installed by Natural Energy).

189

Large instalation of Solaroll on ground to heat the domestic hot water for the Bahama Princess hotel in Bermuda.

Solaroll on the roof of another Bahama Princess hotel to heat the water in their large swimming pool at the hotel. I am checking on the instalation).

A new school in north N.J where radiant heat was used to heat the school.

SolaRoll tubing was placed on the ground and concrete poured on top to act as a radiant heated floor. Hot water is pumped thru the SolaRoll tubing.

Photo shows SolaRoll tubing going from one room to another.

The
Courier-News

Local

B1

Friday March 4, 1983

Bridgewater is told sun can cut pool costs

By JOSEPH R. PERONE
Courier-News Staff Writer

BRIDGEWATER — Heating coils on the roof of the municipal pool could be used to keep swimmers warm, and possibly save money if township officials decide to take the plunge into solar energy.

The township Redevelopment Agency listened intently last night as the representative of a New York firm explained a novel way of using a solar heating unit that would cost the township nothing to install and reduce the pool's water heating bill by 20 percent.

Private investors would pay for installing the system, which would cost about $183,000, and the township wouldn't have to put up a dime, according to William S. Bunte, who represents Bio-Energy Services Corp. of Ellenville, N.Y.

Bunte, who lives at 8 Brian Drive and is the president of Natural Energy Sales & Consultants Inc., told the agency that private investors would pay for the system and use it as a tax shelter and that Bio-Energy Services Corp. would handle all maintenance.

The township's only part would be to use the system for 10 years, after which it could buy the system outright at a depreciated price or extend the contract. The township still would pay operating costs, but Bunte said he would guarantee that the township would save about $3,000 in heating costs.

"We do all the maintenance and they (township residents) would be guaranteed a 20 percent savings," he said.

Bunte explained that the system would work like this: synthetic rubber heating coils, with a life of 30 to 50 years, would be glued to the roof of the pool. Water would run through the coils, gain heat from the sun and then flow to an advanced heating pump that would be used to heat water in the pool.

The special pump can extract heat from the air even at night and even when the temperature is minus 10 degrees Fahrenheit, according to Bunte. He said other heating pumps can extract heat from the air only when the outside temperature is 40 degrees or higher.

Bunte said Overlook Hospital in Summit and St. Peter's Medical Center in New Brunswick also are considering using the solar heating system because they use large amounts of water.

"It sounds like a fantastic thing for the township," said Kurt Shadle, member of the Redevelopment agency. The agency plans to consider the proposal, but did not set a date for making a decision.

The Redevelopment Agency also heard a proposal from a North Plainfield firm that claims its infrared, natural gas heaters could heat the pool building and save 50 percent in energy each year. Currently, the pool building uses oil heat.

Mark McIntosh, president of McIntosh Associates Inc., told the agency that his firm could supply the township with a natural gas system that would provide more than 2 million British thermal units of heat for about $16,000. He said the township could save money by having its employees install the units under the supervision of his firm.

McIntosh, who is a member of the pool, said the yearly operating costs would be about $15,000, which he believes is about half of what the township currently pays.

It turns out that the Bridgewater Swim Club did not purchase either system. I visited the pool on June 17, 2004 and found that they are still using the oil heater to heat the pool. The Director of the Club said that they have some problems with the system...

Natural Energy booth at the Energy Show (I am manning the booth).

MINUTES OF SPECIAL MEETING OF SHAREHOLDERS
OF BIO ENERGY SYSTEMS, INC.

Minutes of Special Meeting of the Shareholders of BIO-ENERGY SYSTEMS, INC., held at the offices of Berger and Friedman, Esqs., 129 South Main Street, Ellenville, New York, on the 7th day of November, 1980 at 10:00 A.M.

Mr. Michael F. Zinn, President of the Company called the meeting to order and acted as Chairman thereof and Steven E. Krulick, Secretary of the Company, acted as Secretary.

The Secretary called the roll and the following Shareholders were found to be present, in person or by proxy:

MICHAEL F. ZIHN	STEVEN E. KRULICK
RONALD W. LEONARD	ERIC T. ZINN
TODD E. EFFREN	WILLIAM BUNTE
SEYMOUR COHEN	LORRAINE T. COHEN
HAROLD HARRIS	WILLIAM G. KENNEDY
MORTON SCHIFF	

The Secretary reported that Shareholders appearing either in person or by proxy represented more than two-thirds of the outstanding shares entitled to vote on proposals presented at the meeting.

The Secretary presented to the meeting a Consent and Waiver of Notice of Special Meeting executed by all the Shareholders of the Company and the same was ordered appended to the minutes of this meeting.

Non-assessable shares of common stock of Corporation of the par value of $.01 each, and each holder of record of a certificate for one or more shares of common stock of the Corporation as of the close of business on the date this amendment becomes effective shall be entitled to receive as soon as practicable and upon surrender of such certificate, a certificate or certificates representing <u>18,809. 91 shares of common stock for each one share of common stock represented by the certificate of such holder,</u> provided that no fractional share shall result and any fractional interest in a share shall be disregarded.

Natural Energy also sold cogeneration equipment* distributed by BESI Corp, and by Concept Tech (Such as the "TECOGEN" shown below).
*Both hot water and electricity are produced from natural gas only

    After about one year of sales the Besi Corp* was so profitable, that their stock split " 18,809.91 to 1"! The stock still kept going up until at one point I found that I was a millionaire (on paper). The only problem was that none of the original eleven investors could sell any of the their shares for three years.... Before the three years was up, the oil shortage was over, and solar sales almost stopped. The Besi Corp stock fell so far, that by the time I could sell my stock, I just barely got my $4,000. investment back. Being rich was not one of my high priorities, and it may have adversely affected my close relationship with God, so it was just an experience as far as I was concerned...

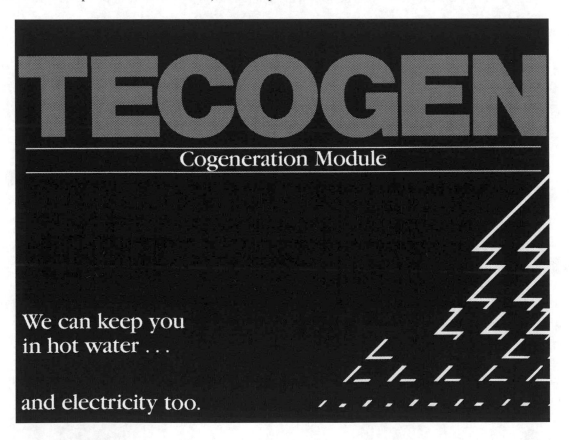

---

*   Also called "Bio-Energy Systems"

May 25, 1989
Mr. William S. Bunte

March 4, 1988

Mr. William S. Bunte
William S. Bunte Consultants
22 Holly Glen Lane North
Berkeley Heights, NJ 07922

Dear Bill:

This letter will summarize our discussion today and the agreement reached between us.

Concept Technology, Inc. will assume all sales responsibilities from this date on for those prospects which you have established, per the attached list.

Concept Technology, Inc. will pay you a commission of $50.00 per kW on any sale to any of those prospects on the attached list which CTI closes between the date of this letter and September 4, 1988. Concept Technology, Inc. will pay you a commission of $25.00 per kW on any such sale which CTI closes between September 5, 1988 and March 3, 1989. After March 3, 1989, all remaining prospects are subject to no commission should a sale occur following that date.

Commissions will be paid, as they have in the past, within thirty days, commensurate with CTI's receipt of funds from the customer.

A residual commission totaling $2,000.00 from the Red Bank YMCA job will be paid to you commensurate with CTI's receipt of funds from its operating contract with Synergics, Inc. The commission will accrue at a rate of $0.50 per operating hour for each hour in excess of 5,000 hours each year.

A final commission totaling $1,005.00 is due you for the Grandview Terrace job. This will be paid to you commensurate with CTI's receipt of funds.

Your responsibilities to earn the above commissions are to maintain the good name of Concept Technology, Inc. and to make yourself available to answer any questions should we need to communicate with regard to the prospects listed.

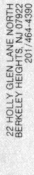

William S. Bunte
Authorized Representative

22 HOLLY GLEN LANE NORTH
BERKELEY HEIGHTS, NJ 07922
201/464-4390

221 CANAL STREET
ELLENVILLE, NY 12428
914/647-6700

BESCO
A BESICORP COMPANY

Overlook Hospital was one
of My customers.

BESICORP

BESICORP GROUP INC., Box 191, Ellenville, N.Y. 12428 (914) 647-6700   TWX 510 240 8340   CABLE: BIOENERGY ELVE

NEWS RELEASE

FOR IMMEDIATE RELEASE

Contact: Michael F. Zinn
(914) 647-6700

BESICORP GROUP INC. RECEIVES MAJOR
HOSPITAL ENERGY SUPPLY AGREEMENT

ELLENVILLE, New York, May 20, 1983—BESICORP GROUP INC. (NASDAQ SYMBOL: BESI), announced today receipt of an energy supply agreement with OVERLOOK HOSPITAL of Summit, New Jersey, for purchase of heated water and steam to the OVERLOOK facility. This new contract, expected to be worth a minimum of two million dollars to BESICORP is the first major hospital to contract with BESICORP under its Solar Thermal Service Plan.

This project is also BESICORP's first use of a special integrated solar energy system designed by BESICORP for use at large energy-using hospitals.

Overlook Hospital was one
of   My   customers.

195

Chapter 9(g)

WSB Funding

As noted under "Second Marriage", I went to Florida to learn about "Factoring" and to obtain my Certificate showing that I was qualified to act as a Factor.

Factoring is for companies (example - company "A") who make a product and sell it to another company "B". Company "B" is short of money and they are not able to pay Company "A" for 40 to 60 days after the product was delivered. Company "A" needs the money sooner, so they contact a Factor. The Factor will take over the invoices of company "A" and pay company "B" for the invoice amounts within a few days (for a fee). The Factor would then receive the payment for the invoices in 30 to 60 days. I would receive a commission from the Factor.

I did some Factoring, but at the time the economy was very good, and most companies did not need this service. Because of this, there were many Factors trying to get the few jobs available.

In view of the above, I spent most of my time on another business, "WSB Consultants".

1994 to Present
WSB Funding Services
Position: President
Basking Ridge, New Jersey
Broker for "Factor" (Buy receivables for cash).

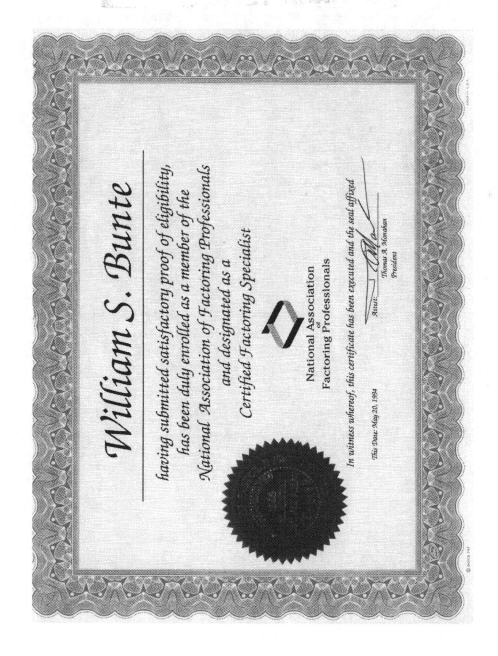

BENEFITS OF FACTORING

1. Elimination of bad debt. A non-recourse factor will assume the risk of bad debt thus eliminating this expense from your income statement.
2. Professional collections. A good factor will handle collections more professionally and more productively than you can. You can eliminate the overhead cost associated with having someone internally handle collections
3. Invoice processing. Factors handle much of the work associated with processing invoices, including mailing them to customers (addressing envelopes, stuffing them, paying for postage), posting invoices to a computer system, depositing checks, entering payments on the computer, and producing regular reports. Again, you can greatly reduce your current overhead cost associated with processing invoices.
4. Offer credit terms to customers. With factoring, you can offer credit terms (or extended credit terms) to your customers without negatively impacting your cash flow. You can grow your business by making it easier for your customers to buy from you.
5. Unlimited capital. Factoring is the only source of financing that grows with your sales. As sales increase, more money becomes immediately available to you. This allows you to constantly be able to meet increasing demand.
6. Take advantage of early payment discounts. Factoring may allow you to take advantage of early payment terms offered by your suppliers. If you can save two percent of your raw materials cost because you have the cash to pay the bills within ten days, this significantly reduces the true cost of factoring.
7. Take advantage of volume discounts. When a company can buy in greater volume from suppliers because of improved cash flow, it will likely save even more money--another direct impact on the bottom line.
8. Stop offering early payment discounts to customers. Many companies offer discounts to customers as incentive to pay the invoices early. Since companies that factor receive their money immediately, they don't need to offer these early payment discounts to their customers. In most cases this discount is at least two percent (sometimes as much as 15%). Factoring will save you every dollar in discounts your customers were taking.
9. Don't give up equity. You do not give up any equity in the company (as is usually required with venture capital) or take on any partners with factoring.
10. Don't incur any debt. Factoring is not a loan and therefore you are not incurring any debt. This keeps your balance sheet looking good, thereby making it easier for you to attain other types of financing or to ultimately sell the company.
11. Factoring helps build credit. Once you begin factoring and you have adequate cash flow, you can begin to pay your bills in a more timely manner and start establishing, or improving, your credit. This improves your chances of getting credit terms from suppliers and improves your chances of getting conventional financing in the future.
© 1995 Cambridge Capital Management, Inc.
12. Factoring is easy and fast. The application required to establish a factoring relationship is much simpler than any other form of financing. No tax returns are needed, no personal financial statements, no business plan, no projections, etc. And, financing usually occurs within one week or so of receipt of contracts. How many banks do you know that operate that quickly?

13. Leverage off your customers credit. A company does not need to be credit worthy to factor. You don't need to be profitable or in business for at least three years, or meet any of the other assorted credit criteria required by banks and other commercial lenders. If you have credit worthy customers, you can get financing through a factor.

14. No personal guarantees. The principals of the company do not have to personally guarantee the repayment of the funding. They usually have to guarantee against fraud or disputes, but not against customers inability to pay. Banks, on the other hand, not only require personal guarantees, they may also require liens on personal assets, such as residences.

15. Detailed management reports. The factor provides you with detailed management reports enabling you to better run your business and manage your cash flow. You no longer have to pay someone internally to produce such reports--another savings.

16. Invoices are paid faster. Many people don't realize that some debtors pay factored invoices faster than non-factored invoices. The reason is that factors generally report payment experiences to Dun & Bradstreet or other credit agencies, and most clients do not. A debtor who is aware of this knows he may impair his credit rating by paying a factor slowly, whereas paying the client slowly may not affect his credit rating at all.

17. Concentrate on marketing and growing the business. As a business owner, you often spend more than half of his time on collections, administration, bookkeeping, fending off suppliers, searching for capital, etc. Factoring frees you up to concentrate on marketing, sales and growing the business. On a more personal note, it can considerably reduce your personal stress level.

18. No geographical limits. A factor can work with a client in any part of the country, and that client can have customers all over the world.

19. Early-warning detection of customer service problems. This benefit is not widely recognized, but is very important. Because factors verify invoices with customers, they discover customer service problems much more quickly than a client would on its own. A non-factoring client will not likely find out about a customer service problem until the invoice goes unpaid and is past due. At this time it's probably too late to salvage the account and the client has probably lost a customer.

Chapter 9(h)

WSB Consultants

I started working as a consultant in sales, marketing, and / or financial areas in 1991. After a while, some of my clients asked me to work part or full time. I started doing this for some friends in 1993 at three to four days per week.

In 2001, I started working 3 days/week at Providet Service. The president, Brian, is a good friend and also a member of The People of Hope. He is great to work for. He gets his available employees together in the morning and leads them in a short prayer. He is also one of the leaders in the Christian Businessmens Assoc. which is sponsored by The People of Hope. I am now (2004) down to 1/2 day per week (at 81 years old). I enjoy working part time and would like to continue, as long as I am needed and as long as my health permits it.

1991 - 1993   WSB Consultants
                   Basking Ridge, New Jersey
                   Position: President
                   Consultant for sales, marketing, and financial (commercial and industrial)

WSB CONSULTANTS
SALES - MARKETING - FINANCIAL
COMMERCIAL & INDUSTRIAL PRODUCTS

William S. Bunte   209 English Place
President   Basking Ridge, N.J. 07920
                                    (908) 647-4641

I am at work at Providet Service Corp. - 2004

METRO DENVER

July 1, 1968   Official Publication of the Denver Chamber of Commerce   Special Issue

EXTRA!   EXTRA!

Kodak Comes to Colorado!

GOOD NEWS TODAY

Big Kodak Plant Planned Near Denver

Eastman Kodak Co. announced Thursday it has acquired an option on 2,400 acres 50 miles north of Denver to build a plant for production of photographic products. Louis K. Eilers, Kodak president, said, "We plan to spend tens of millions of dollars in developing our new Colorado property."*

...another announcement of tremendous significance to all of Colorado....

"... Forward Metro Denver is proud to have provided information and assistance in the establishment of this great new industry. We by no means take complete credit. We extend special appreciation and congratulations to Governor John Love and his staff, the Area Development of the Public Service Company of Colorado and many others who worked long and hard to make this announcement a reality. ..."

Edward F. Kingman, President,
Denver Chamber of Commerce

*Reprinted from the Denver Post.

BUSINESS

Rocky Mountain Enterprises

When I was working for Egan Machinery, Eastman Kodak was one of my customers. One day while I was there on a sales call, I heard some of the employees talking about a new Kodak plant that was going to be built near Windsor, Colorado. He had a sales trip planned to California the following week. I changed my schedule so that I could stop at Denver, Colorado for a few days. I had two brothers, Pat and Jack, who live in Colorado, so we all drove to Windsor when I arrived in Denver. Windsor was a very small towm, and the local people had just heard about the Kodak plant. My brothers knew a real estate agent who covered the Windsor area, so they contacted him. He took them to see the land where the plant was going to be built. The prices for the land had not increased so far.

We decided to buy 250 acres of land just 1/2 mile from Windsor. We put a small down payment to hold the land (and price) until we could form a corporation. With some family members, the real estate agent, and a few friends (including two lawyers), we formed a corporation called "Rocky Mountain Enterprises". In all there were 12 stockholders. The stockholders elected me as the president and we purchased enough shares to take possession of the property. By the time we started selling lots, the price/acre had increased, and kept increasing during the rest of the development. It helped that the real estate Agent bought one of the lots and built a house on it for himself.

When all the lots had been sold, we realized how successful the project had been. For every $1,000 invested by a stockholder, he received $10,000 back!

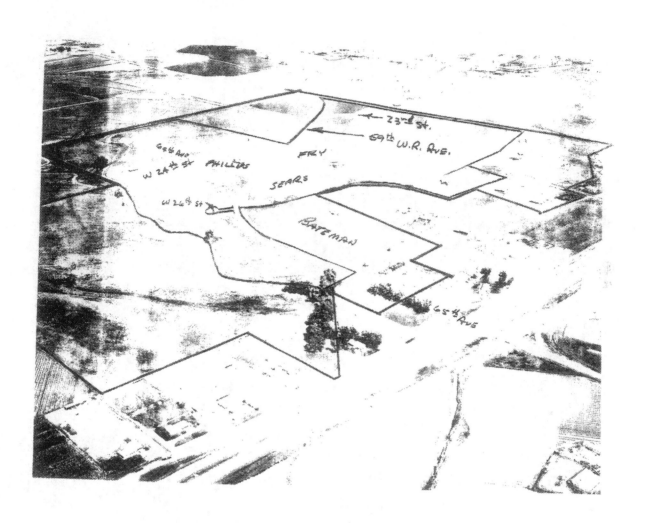

My brother Pat, checking the property layout before selling lots.

ROCKY MOUNTAIN ENTERPRISES OF N.J., INC
77 North Bridge St.
Somerville, N.J.

January 23, 1977

Dear Stockholder:

A dividend of $32,000.00 was approved on January 22, 1977 by
the Board of Directors. The dollar value of the dividend for
each stockholder is shown below:

Stockholder	No. Shares Stock	Dividend
Patrick H. Bunte	54	$1966.00
James A. Gibbons	65	2366.00
Robert H. Folk	65	2366.00
Edward M. Hogan	65	2366.00
Jeremiah J. Hurley	107	3896.00
Janet E. Hurley	54	1966.00
John J. Bunte	54	1966.00
Raymond L. Peterson	95	3458.00
Janice D. Sears	107	3896.00
William S. Bunte	213	7754.00
Total	879	$32000.00

The 107 shares from the Estate of John S. Pitz have been
transfered to Janet E. Hurley and William S. Bunte. The 107
shares from the Estate of Helen S. Bunte have been transfered
to John J. Bunte and William S. Bunte. The 107 shares of
R. Douglas Sears have been transfered to Janice D. Sears.
Your dividend check is enclosed.

Sincerely,

William S. Bunte, Tras.

One of the dividends to the stockholders.

One day in 1987, I saw an ad in the Wall Street Journal for 260 acres for sale only one mile from a new Toyota plant, that was being built near Georgetown, KY. With my experience with Rocky Mountain Enterprises in mind, I called the party that put the ad in the Journal. Based on what he told me, I flew to Lexington and met with the owner of the 260 acres. When I told him (Bill G.), about our experience in Colorado, he said that he would like to do the same thing in Kentucky. He asked if I would be president of the corporation that would be started. We got friends and relatives and did the same thing as we did in Colorado. The land was more expensive in Kentucky than in Colorado, so we had to get more stockholders. We ended up with 28. At the first stockholder's meeting, I was elected president, Bill G. secretary, and Gary G. vice president.

In order to sell lots (one to two acre size) we had to get a layout map made that would show the roads and lot locations. It then had to be approved by the local Planing Board. The Planing Board said that the road, along the front of our property, was not wide enough for the amount of traffic that would be coming from our development. The county said they did not have the money to widen this road. We looked into buying land at the rear of our development, that could connect us to a larger road, but the land was much too expensive. This and other problems took years. We had to obtain a loan from the local bank to meet our expenses (taxes, lawyers, accouantants etc..We obtained permission from the Planing Board to sell 5 acre lots. However, the price of land in the area fell. The Toyota plant was completed by then, but most new workers from Kentucky and other adjoining states decided to commute rather than build near the plant. We even tried an ad in the Wall Street Journal, but no buyers.

At the time I am writing this (June 2004), we have sold a little over half the property, and have a contract with a new buyer to purchase the balance of the property before the end of July 2004. Even if this sale goes thru, the stockholders will not get all of their original investment back.

It has been 17 years since we bought this property. It certainly has not worked out like Colorado!

Photo's of part of the 260 acres.

Toyota builds biggest U.S. plant, still has room to grow

Dodge: The plant will be able to produce at least 200,000 engines annually

The first Kentucky Camrys will be produced next May or June.
—Kusunoki

Toyota plans to add a facility to build engines, axles and steering components to its nearly completed plant

Since this newspaper clipping, the plant has almost doubled in size.+

Chapter 9(i)

KEB Packaging Corp.

Thishis was a small company that did contract packaging. I started out working in the Accounting Dept, and end up as accounting mgr.

It was an interesting job, and was important because it gave some additional financial experience for my future work as a consultant. (WSB Consultants), which included Sales, Marketing, and Financial.

Also most of the employers that I worked with there were friends from The People of Hope community. (I was a member). That made it a great place to work.

1988 - 1990   KEB Packaging Corp.
Carteret, New Jersey
Position: Accounting Manager
Accounts payable, accounts receivable,
and payroll.

Chapter 10(a)

SPIRITUAL LIFE – GENERAL

Let's Pray **Together** —to build family spirit through family prayer

FAITH SHARINGS FROM OUR READERS

Back on Trinity Sunday we asked you to help us enrich our understanding of God by sharing with us your reflections on the Trinity. Many of you responded, and we want to publish some of your thoughts each week in the next few issues of TOGETHER. Some letters were quite long, so we have excerpted portions to print. Our wholehearted thanks to all who wrote.

Rose Weninger of Anamoose, North Dakota writes: "The terminology chosen to describe God's existence in the Trinity–three persons in one–is more than that to me. It is also a definition of God's existence through time: the past, present and future. God has continually given us assurance that He was, is and always will be. The sending of God, the son, by God Himself proves to me God was and is. The continuing daily miracles through God, the Spirit, proves to me He is and always will be. His promises were living through our ancestors, are living through us, and will continue to live through our children."

From Jane Brink Ft. Myers Beach, Florida: "God the Father called forth the light or the life-giving energy Source, the Holy Spirit. When perfect thought united with pure energy, physical manifestation was the result, and God created. Thus Jesus Christ came from God and was worthy to return to God, thereby opening heaven to all."

Sister Mary Roxette Lambert of ??? New Hampshire: "God is Infinite Love and although One, cannot remain alone. His love is diffusive. The Father eternally begets the Son and their mutual love is the Spirit . . . It is as simple as what St. John tells us: 'God is Love.'"

William S. Bunte, Berkeley Heights, New Jersey "The idea that the Father, Son and Holy Spirit are three persons but only one God is, of course, a mystery. After praying about it I did get the following thought: The Father, Son and Holy Spirit are so close to each other in all their spiritual thoughts, words and actions, that they are truly one–somewhat like a man and woman become one when they marry. Jesus acknowledges this in John 14:11: 'You must believe me when I say that I am in the Father and the Father is in me.'"

Margaret Tarker writes from Lebanon, Pennsylvania: "The Blessed Trinity is something to ponder–a mystery that not even the greatest detective could analyze. Believing is so much easier."

Immaculate Conception Rectory
35 MOUNTAIN AVENUE
SOMERVILLE. N. J. 08876

P.O. Box 956

April 10, 1980

Mr. William S. Bunte'
8 Brian Drive
Bridgewater, N. J. 08807

Dear Bill,

It would make me very happy if you would be willing to serve as an <u>Extraordinary</u> <u>Minister</u> of Holy Communion.

I am sure that Our Lord would never suffer any careless indignity at your hands. Your reverence for Our Eucharistic Lord would be a great service to us.

If you should have any uneasiness about it, call me to discuss it. Hopefully, you will be able to respond in the affirmative so we can arrange a suitable ceremony with Father Cicerale.

Gratefully and devotedly,

Rev. Msgr. Eugene B. Kelly

Thousands rally in Trenton to oppose abortion

By DAVID VANHORN

New Jerseyans yesterday paraded placards and raised their voices in ernnation of abortion and in support of the rights of the unborn at a ly for Life" in Trenton.

Carrying homemade signs and ers and singing songs such as "God ; America," the crowd marched al blocks to the steps of the State-?. There, more than 20 speakers, ding politicians, clergymen and ife leaders, implored for an end to ized abortion.

"We have the truth on our side," Molly Kelly, executive director of sylvanians for Human Life. "We the youth on our side and we have on our side. God never loses."

Some 10,000 people attended the ring, making it the largest pro-life in state history, said John To-i, executive director of the New y Right to Life Committee. State e, however, estimated that 7,000 e attended. They said there were cidents.

The crowd of tots, teens, colle-, parents and senior citizens car-a plethora of signs. Many slogans .ed abortion with genocide, such as rtion is Murder," "Murder used to ainst the law," "Pro-choice is pro-." and "Put your baby in a crib, . casket." Others said "Don't put .ork out of business," "What about .aby's choice?" and "Abortion is birth control."

Two marchers, Dominic Caruso, n accountant from Pennsauken, tose McCarthy, 68, of River Edge, ared abortion to the killing of by the Nazis during World War II. re got a holocaust right here in our country," Caruso said.

McCarthy was attending her first "I've always been afraid to get he crowd but I thought it was time . counted," she said.

Using the Statehouse as a stage symbolic gesture because pro-life rs hope the state Legislature will .aws to restrict abortions, demon-rs noted. Tomicki said he is opti-: that legislators will approve a nat requires parental notification ortions for women under age 18.

'We are at the state Capitol, right nt of the heart of state govern-in New Jersey, and you have spo-ut," said Richard Traynor, presi-

Associated Press

Anti-abortion demonstrators, some with their children, gather in front of the Statehouse during a rally

dent of the New Jersey Right to Life Committee. "New Jersey is pro-life."

Kelly told demonstrators New Jersey is a key battleground on abortion, "and the rest of the world is watching you."

"We want abortions restrictions here in New Jersey," said Marie Ransome, state director of Concerned Women for America, and the crowd applauded.

Ransome disagreed with claims that poor people are getting most abortions, noting that 93 percent of abortions are "because of inconvenience."

"I came from a family of 17 children," she said. "We were poor but proud. Pro-abortionists want us to kill our babies for economic reasons; it's as simple as that."

Other speakers agreed that abortion has become a "big business" and

said there have been 25 million abortions in the United States since the Supreme Court legalized abortion in 197: in Roe vs. Wade.

"The stench of death hangs heavy over this nation," said Kelly, who called abortion clinics "killing institutions."

Tomicki reminded the crowd tha a judge in Tennessee last week ruled that life begins at conception in a case involving custody of seven frozen embryos. The belief that life begins at conception was one of many popular themes at the rally.

"At every single point, life is precious and sacred," said the Most Rev James McHugh, bishop of the Diocese of Camden.

McHugh said Roe vs. Wade lacked clear legal reasoning and failed politically because the American public is uncomfortable with abortion on demand. A recent U.S. Supreme Court decision on abortion gives New Jersey and other states a chance to reassess protection of the unborn, he said.

Vera Roche, state director of the Eagle Forum, said, "We're on a roll now and we'll continue until we roll back Roe vs. Wade."

But several leaders stressed that the pro-life movement has an uphill battle because of the money, political pressure and sympathy from the media that supporters of legal abortion can muster.

"I just hope the press doesn't underplay all of this in the paper tomorrow," said Sandra Bobinski, state president of the Columbiettes, the ladies' auxiliary to the Knights of Columbus.

The state deputy for the New Jersey State Council of the Knights of Columbus asked the crowd to join pro-life groups and not to become complacent after the rally ends.

"Don't fall for the trap that this is the end," Dominic Calabrese said.

Calabrese also noted that pro-abortion forces will be rallying in Trenton next month. "Who cares?" he said. "If they come in with 6 million people, that proves that 6 million people are wrong. We know we are right."

Rep. Christopher Smith (R-4th Dist.) called today's pro-life supporters "modern-day abolitionists." Pregnant women need "positive alternatives" to abortion, such as prenatal care and adoption services, he said.

"I believe the winds of change are blowing, and the winds of reform are blowing," Smith said.

Even though the subject at hand was serious, the rally did have its lighter moments.

"As soon as this is over, you're invited to my place for pizza," joked Brian Rechten, founder and president of Americans Concerned for Tomorrow.

We were there!

William S. Bunte

Prophecy

Recently I had a Prophecy from the Holy Spirit that seemed a little "odd". However, after I really thought about it, I saw a much deeper meaning.

The Prophecy was :

"If you should die with unconfessed serious sin, have you really thought about what eternity means. Imagine a large rocket ship that takes 100 lbs of the earth to the largest planet (Jupiter*) and then returns to earth to pick up another 100 lbs, and keeps doing this until "all" of the earth is on the other planet. At that point, eternity has just begun... For those who don't believe in me, or those who believe but live in serious sin, have you made the wrong choice?"

This means that our time on earth is very, very short compared with eternity "forever".

---

*   Jupiter is 10.9 times larger than earth and 483,000,000 miles from earth.

Chapter 10(b)

Charity

I always tried to tithe, with the larger amounts going to my local church (St James), The People of Hope and their school (Koinonia Academy), and the balance to about twenty misc. charities (such as: Asian Relief, Food For The Poor, Catholic Medical Mission, N.J. Right To Life, Morality Media, Prison Fellowship, etc.

When I was working for myself or companies who paid fairly high salaries, I would also put additional funds into the following charities (when the exta funds were available):

Gift Annuities:

Since I never worked for a company long enough to obtain a pension, I put a certain amount of my savings into gift annuities for the following reasons: (1) They paid a high interest rate (6 to 9 percent for men in the 65 to 80 age bracket (the older the higher the rate), and (2) approximately 50% of the investment profits went the charity that sponsored the annuity (say "Covenant House", or "Catholic Relief Services", and the other 50 % would come to me (monthly) for the rest of my life. At the end of my life 100% of the interest payments would go to the charity.

Besides Covenant House and Catholic Relief Services, I also have Gift Annuities with two other charities. Without these annuities, I would only have my Social Security and a small amount from my part time job, and I would not be able to live in this high cost area.

"I give thanks to my God in every prayer I utter, rejoicing, as I plead on your behalf, at the way you have helped promote the Gospel from the very first day."

Phil 1:3-5

Come Lord Jesus

Certificate of Appreciation

Mr. & Mrs. William Bunte

With gratitude to Almighty God, I give thanks for your generous support of the apostolic work and pastoral ministry in the Local Church. Through Forward In Faith you have helped to enrich the spiritual and temporal welfare of the Diocese of Metuchen.

May God bless you.

Most Reverend
Theodore E. McCarrick
Bishop of Metuchen

218

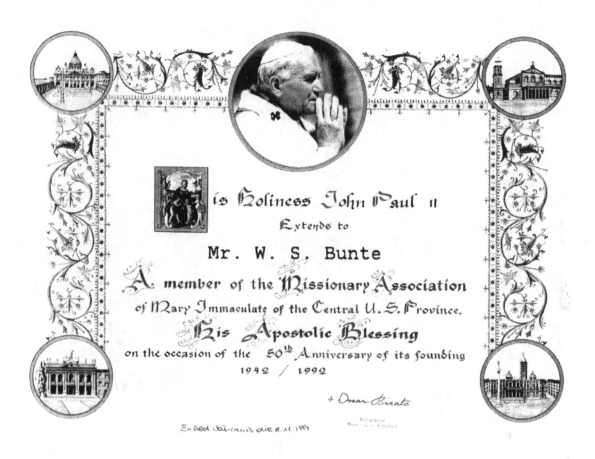

His Holiness John Paul II

Extends to

Mr. W. S. Bunte

A member of the Missionary Association

of Mary Immaculate of the Central U. S. Province.

His Apostolic Blessing

on the occasion of the 50ᵗʰ Anniversary of its founding

1942 / 1992

This Certificate of Appreciation

is presented to

Mr. William S. Bunte

a "Disciple in Service"

in recognition of outstanding dedication
to the worldwide missionary work
of

MISSIONHURST — CICM

"The harvest is rich,
but the workers are few."
Luke 10:2

Rev. Joe Giordano, CICM
Missionhurst

TENTH ANNIVERSARY

CERTIFICATE OF APPRECIATION

This Certifies That

Mr. William Bunte

*Is a faithful contributor to Prison Fellowship, helping to bring the news of God's love
and forgiveness to prison inmates.*

And has generously renewed that support as we enter our second decade of ministry.

Charles W. Colson, Chairman

August 15, 1986

PRISON
FELLOWSHIP
MINISTRIES
TENTH
ANNIVERSARY
1976 · to · 1986

In grateful recognition of extraordinary commitment to disadvantaged youth
and the mission of Covenant House

WILLIAM S. BUNTE

CHARTER MEMBER
COVENANT HOUSE

CORNERSTONE

April 9, 1997
Date

Sister Mary Rose McGeady, D.C.
President, Covenant House

"I bound myself by oath, I made a covenant with you ... and you became mine." —Ezekiel 16:8

220

Uniform Gift Annuity Rates Single Life			
Age	Rate	Age	Rate
55	5.5%	73	6.8
56	5.6	74	6.9
57	5.6	75	7.1
58	5.7	76	7.2
59	5.7	77	7.4
60	5.7	78	7.6
61	5.8	79	7.8
62	5.9	80	8.0
63	5.9	81	8.3
64	6.0	82	8.5
65	6.0	83	8.8
66	6.1	84	9.2
67	6.2	85	9.5
68	6.3	86	9.9
69	6.4	87	10.2
70	6.5	88	10.6
71	6.6	89	11.0
72	6.7	90	11.3
			and over

BRIGHTER FUTURES SOCIETY

William S. Bunte

IN APPRECIATION FOR YOUR SPECIAL HELP

THROUGH YOUR ESTATE PLAN

CHILDREACH

THANKS YOU

FOR HELPING TO BUILD A BRIGHTER FUTURE

FOR OUR WORLD'S POOREST CHILDREN

CHAIRMAN, BOARD OF DIRECTORS

Founded in 1937 as Foster Parents Plan

19 85

FRIENDS OF SOS CHILDREN'S VILLAGES, INC.

Providing a home, a family and education for needy
children throughout the world since 1949

Certificate of Appreciation

awarded to

WILLIAM S. BUNTE

...whose generous support during 1985 helped us through two of the worst disasters in history, and
whose love for children gives us the hope for better things to come for all homeless children throughout
the world.

President

June 30, 2004

COVENANT HOUSE
PLANNED GIVING
346 WEST 17TH STREET, NEW YORK, N.Y. 10011-5002
(212) 727-4110   Fax: (212) 727-4964

William S. Bunte
209 English Place
Basking Ridge, NJ 07920

Dear Bill,

It is a pleasure to again enclose your latest payment of $198.43 from your Covenant House Gift Annuity which you established on October 27, 1992. Thank you again for this generous gift.

Yes, the kids keep on coming. And we're still here for them.

For the past year, I've been a volunteer mentor - sort of a "big brother" - for young men living at Covenant House. I'm on my second kid now and the experience is valuable for both of us. I get to help a few kids directly and deepen my understanding of our mission, and the kids get immeasurable benefits from relating to and being recognized by a 'well adjusted' normal adult. They see what success looks like, which helps them visualize their own future success.

Some of our kids are very bright. I played chess with my current mentee, Eric, last week, and I'd like to think beating me was a challenge for him. I should practice more!

Eric is working two jobs, trying to save up money to start a business as a house painter. He's motivated and focussed. With a little luck and Covenant House behind him, he has a real chance to succeed. I'll do my best to play my part.

Thank you, Bill, for playing your part, too.

Gratefully,

Norm Lotz

Enc: Check

Chapter 10(c)

Foster Parents Plan

I started with the Foster Parents Plan in 1960. With this Plan, I would "adopt" a poor child in a foreign country and help with their living expenses by sending a monthly check to the Plan. I would also write a letter to the child to go along with the check. The child (or the Plan's contact person assigned to the child) would write a letter back to me. Although the money was supposedly just for the child, it actually helped the entire family.

My first child was "Dinh Van Duy Long" (Long was actually his first name). Long was from Vietnam (before the war with North Vietnam). Long's father was a fisherman and a photographer. Long sent me same beautiful photos of fishing boats taken by his father. We exchanged letters until the war started, and then Foster Parents had to stop their operation. After the war was over, I contacted Foster Parents to see what happened to Long, but they were not able to locate him.

There have been many foster children since Long and from many countries including Mexico, Brazil, and other South American countries. It has been a very rewarding experience for me.

Ding VAn Duey Long with mother and sister (Photo - left - 1964, and right - 1967).

Parade in Vietnam (Photo sent by Long).

Long with father and sister.

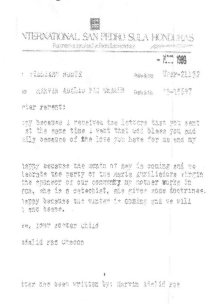

This foster child (Marvin) is from Honduras. (Another letter from Marvin is on next page).

NTERNATIONAL SAN PEDRO SULA HONDURAS

'Mr. W. S. Bunte   US 021152

Maarvin Adalid Paz   39-15697

                    August 22, 1989

ster Parent:

th love and with kindly I'm sending you in
ords all class of happiness, for all the fa-
d that God bless you and help you with your

ll, we are fine with health and we are enjoying
e beautiful summer we are having here in my
y.

wish you the bes with all the love.

                    Your foster child,

                    Marvin Paz

Chapter 10(d)

Volunteering

Nursing Home

I heard that Jim Campblell was at Greenfield Convalescent Center in Bridgewater, NJ. Jim used to work for me when I worked at Union Carbide Corp. I went to visit Jim in 1979, and found that he had Multiple Sclerosis. I started visiting Jim about once a week. One day the owner of the Center asked if I (and my wife, if posible) could come every Saturday morning and help. All the patients that could would come to a large TV room where we would serve them coffee, tea, and cookies, and talk to them individually. Lorna and I decided to try it. We would also come to help at special parties.

The owner found out that I was a Eucharistic Minister for the local Catholic Church. She asked if I would be willing to bring the Eucharist once a week to the Catholics that would like to receive it. I asked the pastor at our church, and he said yes, as long as I wore the same black robes that we wore at Mass (When we distributed the Eucharist). Although I told the people that I was not a priest, several of the older women would ask me to hear their confession every time I came!

Couple named volunteer finalists

BRIDGEWATER – – Mr. & Mrs. William Bunte of 8 Brian Drive were awarded a certificate to acknowledge them as finalists in the Volunteer of the Year competition conducted by the New Jersey Association of Health Care Facilities.

The Buntes, who were honored as Greenfield Convalescent Center's Volunteers of the Year in May 1982, have been volunteers at the center for over five years. During this time, they have shared their experiences and given of their time to Greenfield residents at Saturday morning coffee hours, weekly church services and with personal visitations to residents who cannot attend functions. Mrs. Bunte also has helped with recreational activities and art classes on a regular basis.

Bunte is the president of Automatic Industrial Machines Inc. in Lodi. His wife is a local artist and a member of the Raritan Valley Art Association.

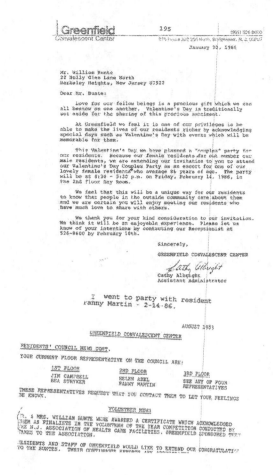

I went to party with resident Fanny Martin - 2-14-86.

August 1983

GREENFIELD CONVALESCENT CENTER

RESIDENTS' COUNCIL NEWS CONT.

YOUR CURRENT FLOOR REPRESENTATIVE ON THE COUNCIL ARE:

1ST FLOOR	2ND FLOOR	3RD FLOOR
JIM CAMPBELL	HELEN ABEL	SEE ANY OF FOUR
BEA STRYKER	FANNY MARTIN	REPRESENTATIVES

THESE REPRESENTATIVES REQUEST THAT YOU CONTACT THEM TO LET YORU FEELINGS BE KNOWN.

<u>VOLUNTEER NEWS</u>

MR. & MRS. WILLIAM BUNTE WERE AWARDED A CERTIFICATE WHICH ACKNOWLEDGED THEM AS FINALISTS IN THE VOLUNTEER OF THE YEAR COMPETITION CONDUCTED BY THE N.J. ASSOCIATION OF HEALTH CARE FACILITIES. GREENFIELD SPONSORED THEY NAMES TO THE ASSOCIATION.

PRESIDENTS AND STAFF OF GREENFIELD WOULD LIKE TO EXTEND OUR CONGRATULATIONS TO THE BUNTES. THEIR CONTINUOUS EFFORTS ARE APPRECIATED.

Greenfield Convalescent Center

presents this

Certificate
of Appreciation

for loyal and valuable services
voluntarily given

by *Lillian Bunte*

 signed on *April 28 th*
by *Linda E Ried*

11-1-80

Dear Lorna and Bill,

It has been several years, I imagine, that you have been volunteering at Greenfield and your service to the Center requires many thank-yous that we sometimes fail to give.

Your contributions on the many Saturdays and with the recent church services has truly been appreciated.

We hope to function as a team at Greenfield in providing the best care possible for our residents, which with your dedication and participation has made the feeling even stronger. Bill, please also extend my appreciation to the fellow deacon who participated with you.

Thank you again.

Sincerely,
Cindi Hewitt

When I was selling Solar Heating units, I would give presentations at High Schools on the advantages of Solar Heating, Engineering, as well as small businesses. One such presentation was at Summit High School in 1981.

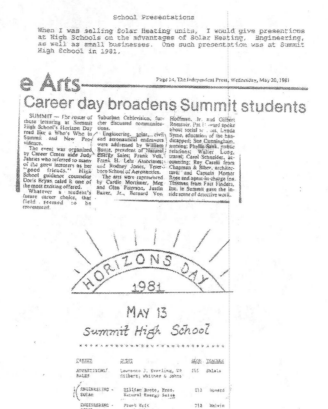

Summit High School

Department of Guidance Services

129 Kent Place Boulevard
Summit, New Jersey 07901
(201) 273-3414

May 20, 1981

Mr. Wiliam Bunte
Natural Energy Sales
115 Dell Glen Ave., Lodi, N.J. 07644

Dear Mr. Bunte,

Thank you for helping make Horizons Day-1981 so successful. The student evaluations are more positive than ever, and the staff enjoyed the people they were able to listen to. Our student's horizons were expanded because of the time, interest, and talent you selflessly devoted to them! We hope your contact with our students was also a rewarding experience for you.

Please extend a special thanks to your business organization for permitting release time from your busy schedule.

Thank you again, and we look forward to having you act as a career resource person in the future.

I was glad you were able to participate. Your presentation has received excellent comments. Enclosed is a slide you forgot and a clipping in today's paper.

Sincerely,

Judy Jahries

Judy Jahries
Career Center Aide

233

Chapter 10(e)

Removal of Objectionable
Reading Materal

In 1963, I joined a committee to help eliminate objectionable reading material in Bridgewater, NJ. (This was a branch of a larger group that covered all of Somerset and Middlesex counties). We would visit the store owners who sold Objectional Literature, and tell them that we are not a censor group, but many of the citizens in their area objected to the sale of this literature. We found that, after visiting the store owners over a two year period, most of them in Bridgewater were willing to cooperate.

January 23, 1966

To: Mayor Leonard B. Galvean
From: William S. Bunte
Subject: Bridgewater Committee For Recent Literature

The Bridgewater Committee For Decent Literature has been very active since it was appointed by you on June 21, 1968. This is a brief progress report on our activities to date.

As previously reported, there are two stores in Bridgewater which had been selling objectional literature which could be harmful if read by children and teenagers. Those stores are:

1) "Sunray Drug Store", Somerville Circle Shopping Center
2) "Franks", Old York Ed.. Bradley Gardens

After several meetings with the managers of these stores and members of our committee, both managers have agreed to cooperate. Periodic visits are made to each store by some member of our committee. Recent visits have shown the Following:

1) "Sunray Drug Store" - 85 to 90% of the objectional magazines, pocketbooks and newspapers have been eliminated from shelves.
2) "Franks" - 90 to 95% of the objectional newspapers, Magazines, and pocketbooks have been eliminated from the shelves.

Both managers of these stores have eventually eliminated the remaining few objectional pieces of literature.

Committee Pushes Drive on Smut

By LOUISE JACOBS

Eleven area stores have removed objectionable reading matter from their newsstands recently as the result of efforts made by a bi-county decent literature committee.

All the cooperating stores are located in Bridgewater and Middlesex Borough. Volunteers assisting the committee are continuing their campaign in 11 other municipalities, but success so far has been meager.

The committee is composed of representatives from Bound Brook, South Bound Brook, Raritan, Green Brook, Somerville, Hillsborough, Manville, Franklin, Bridgewater, Dunellen, Piscataway, and Middlesex.

At Work Two Years

It was organized two years ago after a public meeting during which 200 residents of Middlesex protested the availability of pornography to borough teen-agers. John Krafjack, then Middlesex chairman, is now area chairman of the committee serving Somerset and Middlesex counties.

Some committee members are backed by active hometown organizations, but in other municipalities, such as Somerville, the program has never gotten off the ground.

The central committee takes no part in organizing local groups, but acts instead as a clearing house for information and as a setter of general aims.

Efforts of the group are not limited to obscene literature, nor does the committee, above all, attempt to define what is obscene.

Courts Differ

Supreme courts of various states have differed on that definition; and most attempts to enforce New Jersey's anti-obscenity statute have foundered on the meaning of the word. A recent legislative attempt at a definition, which Senator William E. Ozzard said would have made even the Bible obscene, was vetoed by Governor Hughes.

The area committee lists, instead, eight practices which it considers "objectionable" if followed as a matter of policy by a publication. These are:

glorifying crime or criminals; describing in detail ways to commit criminal acts; holding lawful authority in disrespect; exploiting horror, cruelty, or violence; portraying sex facts offensively; using blasphemous, profane or obscene speech indiscriminately and repeatedly; featuring indecent, lewd or suggestive photographs or illustrations; and holding up to ridicule any national, religious, or racial group.

While definition of some of these points in court might be as difficult as defining obscenity, the committee has no intention of ever taking anyone to court.

Not a Censor Group

"We aren't that type of an organization," said Krafjack. "We aren't a police group and we aren't a censor group. But we think we have a problem here, and we'd be remiss in our duty as citizens if we didn't try to do something about it in a democratic way.

"We try to remind storekeepers that they are upstanding citizens in their communities," he continued. "We appeal to them to play a part which can be respected. If they refuse, we engage in no controversy, and we more or less let the matter drop."

Krafjack said his group has made no attempts to take business away from merchants who will not cooperate.

Types of literature which the committee objects to are not usually exposed to full public view. A recent check of Somerville news stores, however, revealed one displaying tabloids in a front counter with the following headlines: "I Killed My Baby to Hide My Sex Sin;" "This Man Raped Me Under Water," and "Ten Thousand Men Prefer Torture to Love."

Stories inside these tabloids seldom live up to the come-on. Meatier material is available in the rear of some of the stores. Krafjack is particularly anxious to keep such material out of the hands of children. He says his group has no interest in what adults read, except that when such material reaches adults, it is inevitably passed on to children.

"Some of the things the kids carry around with them would make your hair stand up on end," he said. "The things are sold to them through the mails, with no questions asked. If one child sees it, they all see it. And if grownups don't speak up the youngsters figure it's all right, right?"

Krafjack has had some experience with teen-agers through his own two children, and the seventh graders he teaches at St. Joseph's parochial school in Bound Brook.

Group Membership

His organization has no paid members, and is tier political, social, group. Municipal are formed volunteer residents but Krafjack urges all municipal have members from other organizations.

In Middlesex, for when he was chairman vited every church, and civic group in t to be represented o mittee; almost all agreed to do so.

"Our aim is twofold," concluded Krafjack. "We let people know what's on, and to encourage others to stand out in community. I have faith eral good judgment think most of us en what's right once we what's going on."

Legal basis for opposition to some of publications is New Statute 2A:115-2, which one guilty of a mi who shows, sells, or any "obscene or inde or picture to another just cause." New le define the terms is by the Legislature nor Hughes.

CHECKING LITERATURE in campaign to remove pornography from newsstands are members of bi-county decent literature committee. Conferring with the chairman, John Krafjack of Middlesex (left) are Raritan Mayor and Mrs. Tullio Mencaroni, Dominick Buono of Bound Brook and William Bunte of Bridgewater.

—Photo by Rosenthal

Chapter 10(f)

Charismatics

In 1976, a friend invited Lorna and me to a charismatic prayer meeting. We decided to go to see what it was like. At the first meeting, the praying "in tongues" with upraised hands was very different from the way we usually prayed. However, we were impressed with the enthusiasm of the people there, the music, and the teaching. We decided to come back the following week. At the next meeting we found out that we didn't <u>have</u> to pray in tongues or with raised hands. We also started taking a course in how to be "Baptized in the Spirit". After completion of this course, we were "Baptized in the Spirit" and received the "Gift of Tongues".

We also found that we were much more spiritual, and that our prayers seemed to be answered more often. One day I was throwing rocks at a target with my son, and I must have thrown too hard on one throw, because my elbow hurt so bad that I couldn't move it at all. I went to our doctor and he said I had "tennis elbow" and it would take a few weeks before it would be back to normal. (He put my arm in a sling). That night we went to our prayer meeting. Just before going into the church, Lorna said "Let me pray over your elbow". She did, and immediately all of the pain was gone, and I had no trouble moving it in all directions. We have had many other examples of answered prayer since that time.

One other area I discovered during the teachings at some of the prayer meetings, was the importance of the proper priorities in my life. God should be first, wife (if married) second, children third, work fourth, and other areas last. When I examined my life and was honest with myself, I realized that work was really my top priority. This wasn't easy for me to change, but when I did, it made a big difference in my life.

Part of Charismatic Prayer Group at My house on New Years Eve.

Lorna & I at Charismatics prayer.

Part of Charismatic Prayer group at our cabin in the Pocono's, PA.

Chapter 10(g)

Retreats

I have found that retreats have played a big part in my spiritual life.

Shortly after my first marriage, I joined a Knights of Columbus chapter in Plainfield, NJ and advanced to the Fourth Degree. This chapter went to the Loyola House of Retreats in Morristown, NJ once a year. My first year there was 1959. The retreats at Loyola are "silent" retreats. Except for a two hour period on Saturday evening, there is no talking with other men on retreat. They even play religious tapes during meals. The priest leading the retreat would give five or six presentations, and we would meditate on each one for about 30 minutes. There were also "Stations of the Cross", confession, and daily Mass on this three day retreat. I liked the first retreat so much that I have been going there ever year since (except when I was sick}. This year (2004) was my 50th retreat at Loyola.

The People of Hope community that I belong to also have retreats every year. When I joined the community they had two retreats a year, and then in 2000 they went to one retreat per year. These retreats are not silent, but it is nice to have time to discuss the content of the talks with my fellow retreatants plus fellowship with them. I like both forms of these retreats equally well. Since I have joined The People of Hope, I have made 37 retreats there.

There is another type of retreat called "A 30 day Directed Retreat". It is a retreat that is normally given to priests. However, it can also be given to lay Catholics. Father Joe Neville, the priest who was with us on our pilgrimage to the Holy Land, asked me during a retreat if Lorna and I would be interested in going on such a retreat. He would be the director and we would be the only ones on the retreat. Also, it would be once a week for 30 weeks, and approximately one to two hours per meeting. We agreed to try it. At each meeting Father Joe would select a subject God's love, heaven, hell, crucifixion, or a scripture passage to meditate on. We would then write our thoughts from the meditation in our notebooks. By the end of the 30 weeks, we each had notebooks that were full of inspiring meditions. I was amazed the way the thoughts came to me. Many were real insights that I know came from God and helped me to grow spiritually.

Photo of retreatants at Loyola Retreat House - Nov. 1959 (I am top center- under arrow),

Nov. 1976 I am (far right) receiving award for 25 retreats at Loyola.

Gold metal for 50 retreats at Loyola

Chapter 10(h)

I have been trying to eliminate sin in my life as long as I can remember. The devil is a very strong opponent... However, God is much stronger!

There are two areas that, with God's help, I have never sinned:

1) I have never had sex with anyone except with my two wives, and then only while we were married. It hasn't been easy, especially when I was traveling by myself on business all over the United States, and many other countries. It was a shock to find out how many business women I met who tried to get me to sleep with them. It can be very tempting when you are lonely and missing your wife. It took a lot of prayers to resist, and I am sure that being a Daily communicant was and is a great help.

2) The second area was profanity. I decided very early in my life (about the same time I decided to go to daily Mass), that I loved God too much to take his name in vain. There was a lot of profanity in the High School football dressing room, and also in the Navy. I can't remember a single time that I ever used Profanity. Again, this was only possible because of prayer and being a daily communicant.

There was one area that I had problems with, and that was not telling the whole truth. What I would say was not a lie, but what I didn't say was sometimes something that could have made me look bad, or different than I wanted to be thought of. At one of the retreats at Loyola, the priest explained St. Ignatius' method of eliminating sin. I decided to try it.

Ignatius method was to pick one sin and in the morning pray that you will not commit that sin for the next four hours. If you do, you are to repent, and resolve not to commit that sin between lunch and dinner, if you do, you repent again and pray that you don't commit that sin during the night. You do the same thing the next day, and the next, etc. until you no longer commit that sin for a month. Then you pick another sin, and go thru the same procedure. Once a month, you are to go back, using this mothod, to be sure that the first sin is still eliminated.

I tried this method on the above sin. It took several months to eliminate this sin, but it has been eliminated ever since. (I am sure there are other methods that also work, but this one worked best for me on the above sin, and on several others that I have tried it on.) This is not an easy method, but for me, the extra effort was worth it.

Using this method, plus prayers, God's help and daily communion, I am getting "closer" to reaching my goal of being sin free......

Chapter 10(i)

The people of Hope

Lorna and I had grown spiritually through Marriage Encounter and the Charismatics. Even so, we were still looking for a deeper commitment and found it in The People of Hope. Actually, we didn't find it. We didn't even know what a covenant Christian community was at that time. A friend we knew, who was a member of Hope, invited us to attend some of their functions, and after a few months, we knew that this was where we wanted to be. Hope is, in a way, something like the way the early Christians lived. "They lived and prayed together, shared their food and material possessions, and were committed to love and serve one another." From Acts 2:42-47). In the past, I had considered myself to be a good Christian, but my actions didn't always show it.

Belonging to The People of Hope has been a wonderful experience and has given me a great sense of joy and peace.

There are approximately 350 men and women in Hope at this time. The community is divided into "Districts", and each District into "Men's Share Group" and "Women's Share Group" In my present Share Group there are 8 men including a coordinator, and 9 women. We meet once a week and share our lives, pray for each other, and discuss other topics as desired. The entire community also gets together once or twice a month, to pray, listen to a relgious teaching, honor new babies, discuss upcoming events, etc.

The community also has its own school (Koinonia Academy), which has grades one thru high school. It is funded primarily by The People of Hope. It is a Catholic school, but is not funded by the Catholic Diocese. There are approxomately 345 students in the school.

In 1987, approximately 38 members of the People of Hope went to Rome and Medjugorje (see photo). Lorna and I were among those who went.

In Rome, we went to a general audience with Pope John Paul 11, visited St Peter's, and other churches.

We then flew to what used to be Yugoslavia, and then took a bus to Medjugorje. We stayed in a private home (Lorna and I, and another couple - see photo). We had our meals with that family.

JESUS 78
Spiritual gathering at Giant Stadium
(Sponsored by The People of Hope.)

John Paul II at Rome
(I am in back - top right)

We went to Mass every afternoon at St. James church. The Mass started at 4 PM, but we had to get there by 2 PM to get a seat. Originally, the Virgin Mary met with the 6 children on the side of the mountain, however, while we were there, she met with them (now 5) in a separate room in the church just before Mass. The Masses were very holy and inspiring.

One afternoon, five of us were walking to go to Mass. It was a clear bright day. A man in our group said "Look at the sun!". We looked, and the sun dazzled us.

We found that we could look at the sun (without any kind of sun glasses), and it didn't hurt our eyes - even after we looked at it for four to five minutes! It was a real miracle! I was sure that it wasn't possible to take a picture of the sun with our simple camera, but I did take one anyway....

When we returned to New Jersey, I took the roll of film and the camera to the best photography shop in our area "The Photo Lab". I told the manager what happened and the picture of the sun. He said that you cannot take a picture of the sun, especially with the camara I showed him. He said he would develop the roll of film and call me when it was ready, probably in three or four days (I was there on a Saturday). On Sunday he called me and was very excited and asked that I come down to his shop right away! When I arrived at the photo shop, the manager had prints of the sun all over the counter and any other flat areas. He kept saying that you can't take pictures of the sun like this...

Although the incident with the sun noted above was impressive, for me, my growth spiritually was much more rewarding. I feel much closer to God when I pray now, than I ever did before. One of subjects that Mary told the children, was the importance of the daily rosary. Before I went to Medjugore I would say the rosary occasionally, but since then I have averaged about five decades a day.

THE PEOPLE OF HOPE

Let every tongue proclaim
to the glory of God the
Father :

JESUS CHRIST IS LORD !

THE PEOPLE OF HOPE

The People of Hope is a branch of Christ the King Association, an international private association of Christ's Catholic faithful, with members in a variety of different dioceses and parishes throughout New Jersey. It is a covenant community whose members are baptized Roman Catholics who have embraced charismatic spirituality in addition to traditional Catholic devotions. It is a community consecrated to Jesus through Mary, the Mother of Hope.

Membership in The People of Hope comes as an invitation by the Lord to participate in a particular expression of the life of the gospel within the Catholic Church. Community members represent a cross-section of the entire range of Christ's faithful - married couples, families, single parents, lay celibates, single people, priests, nuns, young and old. Members live in a variety of towns, neighborhoods, and living situations and participate and serve in their local parishes. Most of those who work hold secular jobs, ranging from professionals to laborers. A number of younger members attend local universities. Most members experience an initial attraction to the life and spirituality of the community. Then, after an initiation and formation process they discern whether God is calling them to become full, "publicly committed" members of The People of Hope. Full membership calls for commitment to abide by the statutes, order, teachings and agreements of the Community.

THE WAY OF LIFE

The men and women who form The People of Hope desire to enter into a living union with Christ through regular prayer, the study of Sacred Scripture, and frequent participation in the sacraments, especially the Eucharist. Moreover, members desire to enter a relationship with one another characterized by active sacrificial love and a shared life as the basis of a life of mission.

The mission of The People of Hope embraces prayer, evangelization, family life, and celibacy. The covenant of The People of Hope has two key dimensions - members' individual commitments to know, love and serve the Lord, as well as their individual pledges to help one another live for Jesus. Entering the covenant does not require vows; rather, it calls for a response to Jesus' admonition in The Sermon on the Mount, "Say 'yes' when you mean 'yes', and 'no' when you mean 'no'. (MT 5:37)."

The common life of The People of Hope consists of corporate prayer, the sharing of resources, and mutual striving to attain the highest ideals of the gospel and Church teaching. While it is the community's covenant and way of life flowing from its statutes, teachings and agreements that gives it cohesion, it is love that binds the members together.

GROWTH IN HOLINESS

Two of the chief aims of The People of Hope are to respond to the universal call to holiness of Vatican Council II, and to form a faith environment in which members find encouragement to strive for the perfection of charity. There are various components of the community's life - large gatherings of the entire community, various sub-groupings within the larger community, social gatherings, retreats, outreaches, teachings, services, programs, and ministries. The express purpose of each of these is to foster growth in holiness by providing support, encouragement, formation, and inspiration.

Membership, therefore, calls for active participation in the community's life. It calls for striving to reach the rich ideals of Catholicism and to respond to the awesome love of God. In short, it calls for striving for perfection in the way of holiness.

SERVICE TO
THE CHURCH AND THE WORLD

A significant aspect of growth in holiness is service - to the Church, to neighbors, to those in need. Community members are strongly encouraged to share God's gifts and blessings with others, particularly the poor, the defenseless, the imprisoned, the aged, youth, the homeless, and the forgotten.

Since its beginning in May of 1977, The People of Hope community has been actively involved in evangelization as a way of sharing God's gifts and blessings. The People of Hope have run numerous parish missions, several large-scale evangelistic events, men's and women's breakfasts, campus evangelistic programs, youth rallies, conferences, workshops, and retreats for youth and adult men and women, both nationally and internationally. In some cases, single men and women as well as families have moved to foreign countries to help establish evangelistic programs there.

For further information about
The People of Hope
call (908) 647-7579 or write to
The People of Hope
P.O. Box 6411
Warren, NJ 07059

OUTREACHES OF
THE PEOPLE OF HOPE

- Marriage in the Holy Spirit Week-ends

- Life in the Spirit Seminars

- Parish missions

- Renewal Resources (Throughout North America)

- Christian Men's and Women's Breakfasts

- Couples for Christ

- Women's Prison Ministry

- Men's Prison Ministry

Members Volunteer At:

- Soup Kitchens

- Crisis Pregnancy Center

- and other social agencies

Affiliated With:

- Koinonia Academy

- University Christian Outreach

- Marian Aids Ministry

Publications:

- *Songs of Hope,* Vol. 1 & 2 with accompanying cassette tapes

- *Raising Children for Heaven,* Books 1 & 2

has received a particular prophetic word 50 to 100 times from various sources over several years. The gist of the word was that God wanted them to evangelize his little ones and lead them on a journey of faith. He said he would show them how to do this. The group wrote down all the prophetic messages they received. They thought about what these words might mean. They prayed about and discussed ways of putting God's word into practice. They began to study evangelism, and they invited Catholic evangelists into their area. The leaders also shared the message with the pastor of their parish.

In the last few years, the parish began to implement the Rite of Christian Initiation of Adults (RICA) which is the process by which adults are prepared for sacramental entrance into the church. When it was being organized, the pastor remembered the prophetic word the prayer group had been receiving. He asked the prayer group members to form the team for the RCIA. The duties of that team fulfilled the prophetic messages to evangelize newcomers to the Catholic faith and to walk with them on their journey of faith. When a prophetic message cannot be acted on immediately, we should not forget it, but dwell with it so that the Lord can clarify it in the future.

word that has taken root in you, with its power to save you. Act on this word. If all you do is listen to it, you are deceiving yourselves" (James 1:21-22).

Inflexibility can cause us to stagnate for years. Once, members of an inner city prayer group received a call from God to lay down their lives for the poor around them. Though for some years the call was extended to them, they resisted it in fear. So, for the next five years, that group experienced little growth in numbers or in spiritual depth.

Older and wiser national leaders visiting them on one occasion, clearly discerned a rigid attitude in the group. The prophetic word no longer claimed anyone's attention. It had become like background music at the meetings—no one noticed it because it was not loud enough to claim their attention. By not being flexible, we tend to domesticate the prophetic charism. Warm, fuzzy, palatable prophecies then come forth, but we no longer hear the prophetic Jesus speak.

The prophetic charism is not dying. But to revitalize it in our groups and in our daily lives it needs our care and nurture. In addition, we need to grow as prophetic listeners. We can respond best to the voice of God's Holy Spirit when we seek to grow in attitudes of docility, dwelling, and flexibility. Our God will then find us ready and willing to respond to his prophetic word as it comes to us in direct prophecy, in scripture, and in everyday life.

Flexibility is an attitude of being radically open to changing our lives in accordance with the Lord's message to us. At times we must repent of the selfishness and hardness of heart that blind us to God's word. Sometimes God calls us to act on his word immediately, sometimes he expects us to wait. If we remain flexible, we will be willing to do what God tells us, when and how he wants us to do it. "Humbly welcome the

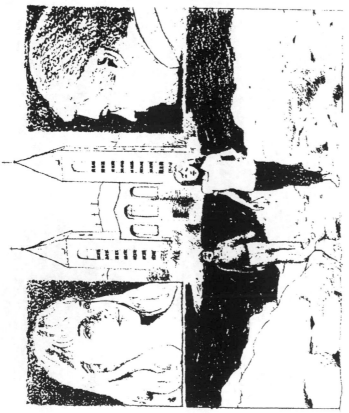

John J. Boucher is a former prayer group leader and parish religious education director. He has contributed a number of articles to New Covenant in recent years.

A Pilgrimage to Medjugorje

An American family travels to Yugoslavia and experiences God's abundant love.

By BRIAN ENGELLAND

Editor's Note: The claimed apparitions of the mother of Jesus to a group of young people in Medjugorje has caused a considerable stir in the Catholic world. Some people believe that God is really giving messages to the human race through these children; others, including the local bishop, believe there is nothing supernatural happening there. Some people have gone so far as to claim it is a case of collective hallucinations.

But almost every one of the thousands of people who have traveled to the little town in Yugoslavia have come back believing that God is indeed doing a spectacular work there. They report of personal conversions and of the spirit of peace and prayer that envelops the town and all who make pilgrimages there.

New Covenant has reported twice before on these claimed apparitions. Our articles have been very popular. People from all over the world have asked us for copies. It is impossible for us to escape the conclusion that this interest has been prompted by a spiritual sense that God is indeed offering direction, hope, and encouragement through the events in Medjugorje.

The article that begins on the next page is one of many firsthand

Members of the People of Hope who went on trip to Rome & Mediugore.
(Photo is in Rome).

Pope John Paul II in Rome right in front of our group.

St James church in Mediugore where the apparitions occurred during our Pilgrimage there.

The inside of the church during the time of the apparitions.

IVAN DRAGIČEVIĆ   IVANKA IVANKOVIĆ   VICKA IVANKOVIĆ
        MARIJA PAVLOVIĆ   JAKOV ČOLO

The children who listen to, and talk to the Blessed Virgin Mary.

The spot on the mountain where the apparitions first appeared.

The cross at the top of the mountain in honor of the apparitions

Going back down the mountain. (You can see St. James church and the town of Medjugorje).

We are talking to one of the visionaries (through an interpreter) at her house.

The Apparitions at MEDJUGORJE

Frances Riehle Rice
President

William A. Rice
Director

Rev. Kenneth J. Sommer, SM
Spiritual Director

BACKGROUND INFORMATION

The place is St. James Parish in the remote village of Medjugorje, Yugoslavia, where it is claimed that the Blessed Virgin Mary has been making almost daily appearances since 1981. Six teenage children (two boys and four girls, ages 10-17) have witnessed the appearances which began June 24, 1981, on a mountain behind the village. The apparition identified herself as the Blessed Virgin Mary, the Queen of Peace.

The message she brings is an urgent one for mankind. She stated to the children, "I have come to tell the world that God exists, and that peace is necessary for the salvation of the world. In God is found true joy from which true peace flows." At another time, she said, "Mankind must be reconciled with God and with one another. For this to happen it is necessary to believe, to pray, to fast, to repent."

THE MESSAGE

The Madonna presents herself as a servant and messenger from God. The messages she brings do not convey any new teachings. They echo the Gospels and teachings of the Church. As at Fatima, they restate the conditions for peace in the world, and for the very existence of the world.

The basic message of Medjugorje is Peace, Conversion, Faith, Prayer, Penance and Fasting. These messages are for the entire world.

Peace – "Peace, peace, peace. Reconcile yourselves!" Several times, Our Lady told the seers that the world is living in great tensions and that it cannot be saved if it continues in this way. The world has to find peace to be saved, but it will not find peace without God.

Conversion – Because of the great decrease in faith and consequent increase of sin in the world, Our Lady has spoken frequently of Medjugorje as a place of conversion which includes reconciliation with both God and mankind.

THE APPARITIONS DESCRIBED

The visionaries see Our Lady as a real three dimensional person whom they can hear and touch. They describe her as beautiful beyond words, radiant with holiness. Her presence is preceded by a brilliant light. Her conversations with the children have taken the form of motherly tenderness and love, and she has taken the role of both Mother and Catechist in advising and directing their lives. She greets them with, "Praise be the Name of Jesus." At the end of the apparition, her last words are always, "Go in the peace of God."

Her apparitions take place daily at the parish about 6:30 in the evening followed by the Rosary and celebration of the Mass with thousands of people in attendance and often with 20 or more priests con-celebrating. The entire service lasts about 3 hours. And this has been happening almost daily since 1981.

THE SECRETS

Our Lady told the children that she would impart ten secrets to all of

Faith – "Have complete faith in God as your Creator; complete reliance on His word." "All mankind has the capacity to know that God exists."

Prayer – "Pray, pray with your hearts." Our Lady specifies praying the spotless Creed, reading scripture, and she says, "The best prayer is the Mass." She encourages group prayer and especially the Rosary. "Open your hearts and come." She explained her role as an intercessor "Pray to Jesus. I am His mother and I intercede with Him. I will help. I will pray with you."

Fasting and Penance – "You have forgotten faith with prayer and fasting you can ward off war and suspend natural laws." The request for penance and reparation for sins is similar to the message of Fatima. At Medjugorje, Our Lady's message that we are on the edge of a catastrophe is the key to understanding the austere request that people feast on bread and water each Friday (those who are physically able). The generous response of the local people in fasting on bread and water is remarkable.

them. Some of these secrets have to do with the world, some with the local church and parish, and some with the Church as a whole. Four of the girls have already received the ten secrets and no longer are. Our Lady, with the others. The other seers have all received nine secrets. The secrets will be revealed only after the Madonna instructs them to do so. We are lead to believe that the coming of a visible sign about 1981 and 1984 seem to speak about.

There have been over a hundred Croatian word for PEACE) written on one evening in large bright letters in the sky above the event. On numerous occasions, thousands have witnessed the sun change colors, spin around a silver-white disc, flash and pulsate in the sky, and throw off a rainbow of colors. There have been physical healings that the most important healings are the deep spiritual changes, the change of hearts and lives in the greatest of all the many "signs" at Medjugorje.

THE GREAT SIGN

One of the secrets, partially revealed by the children, is that Our Lady has promised to leave a visible sign on the mountain where she first appeared, so that the world would believe. The sign will be a testimony, a cause for conversion among those who do not believe Our Lady said, "You must not wait for the sign before you convert yourselves, don't delay." She said that the sign would be given in time of grace for you. This is a time of grace. Most of the children's apparitions. Most of the children know what the sign will be and the exact date.

UNUSUAL EVENTS AND WONDERS

Unusual events began taking place soon after the first apparition. A large number of these have to do with the large crosses at the top of Mount Krizevac, one of the highest mountains surrounding the valley. In 1933, a 33 foot concrete cross was erected on the mountain by the

people to commemorate the 1900th year of our Lord's death and resurrection. A most noteworthy sign was the word "MIR" (the

THE CHURCH'S POSITION

The appearances of Mary on earth which have been approved by the Catholic Church have the following points in common:

1) Mary calls us back to God, a return to Jesus.
2) Mary reaffirms what is already in the Faith and teachings of the Catholic Church.
3) Mary calls us to prayer and sacrifice in reparation for sin, a message of the Gospels.

All these points are present at Medjugorje.

Following the closing of an investigative commission headed by the local Bishop of Mostar, the Congregation for the Doctrine of the Faith in Rome in January 1987 established a new commission (on a national level) to study the events at Medjugorje.

THE RIEHLE FOUNDATION

The Riehle Foundation, founded in 1977, is a tax-exempt non-profit foundation distributing Catholic and other Christian literature around the world. Books, Bibles, rosaries, etc. are free to missions and seminaries in third world countries, to prison chaplains, schools, groups and individuals. The foundation, to Our Lady of Fatima, April 11, 1985. Eleanora died at age 83; Ray died at age 69 on October 13, 1986 (the same date of the miracle of the sun at Fatima in 1917.)

After his death, their daughter Frances, and her husband, Bill, continued operating the foundation. The foundation is still deeply committed to making known Our Lord's message of love and peace being delivered through His Mother Mary, and now that message assurance to be coming from Medjugorje. We thank you for your prayers and support.

Medjugorje.

The Riehle Foundation recognizes and accepts that the final authority regarding the apparitions at Medjugorje rests with the Holy See of Rome, to whose judgement we willingly defer.

SUMMARY

St. James Parish in Medjugorje is the center of all activity. All services and devotions center around the Parish. Mary affirms this with, "Return to Mass." Father Tomislav Pervan, the Pastor of St. James senses that to truly all work in his parish through Mary's intercession. He brings Christ. People find God here, in the Mass, in the Sacrament of Reconciliation, a return to faith that is the biggest miracle.

Crowds of pilgrims continue to flock to Medjugorje over five million to date. They come to this tiny village that initially had no public facilities, no restaurants or lodging. People of all faiths come and join together in prayer.

The apparitions continue daily, the length of the appearances have (seems of shorter duration.

The visionaries with only 2 or 3 of the secrets have to be convinced, while there are a lot of people still come and respond to her message. It is urgent message of love, peace and hope for conversion and reparation; an event unfolding in a mountain village in a Communist country, a brutal delivered by the Handmaid of the Lord.

"The Apparitions at Medjugorje Prolonged"
By Fr. Rene Laurentin

A 116 page book with updated information into 1987.

Why has the unveiling of the 10 secrets not yet begun? Is it merciful delay?

What about the seers; the health of Vicka; Ivan in the military service? Ivern of Helena and Marijana and Jakov; the young people's prayer group. What of the Church's position and the Bishop's Commission?

For a copy, write: The Riehle Foundation
P.O. Box 7
Milford, Ohio 45150 U.S.A.
(513) 528-3588

Suggested donation: $5.50 (includes postage)

258

Eating dinner at the house where we stayed (Lorna first on right, the other Hope couple on the left - first and third. The other two women live in the house. (I took the picture)

Chapter 11

Misc.

Bound Brook Adult School

Bound Brook, N. J.

This is to Certify, That ___MR. WILLIAM BUNTE___ has

successfully completed _20_ hours of training in ___SPEED READING___

and is therefore awarded this Certificate ___DECEMBER 5___ 19 _66_

Eugene B. Stottlman
Instructor

Jos Donnelly
Director

George H. Daniel
Superintendent of Schools

Lorma & I (right of center) with friends (and others) on a tour
thru Howe Caverns in New York State (8-13-92).

Congress of the United States
House of Representatives
Washington, D.C. 20515
December 6, 1976

Mr. William S. Bunte
8 Brian Drive
Bridgewater, N.J. 08807

Dear Mr. Bunte:

Thank you for your recent note and for
sending me a copy of McKeever's investment letter.

Many of the allegations which Mr.
McKeever reports are indeed startling and I
will certainly check out his allegations about
nuclear weapons off the U.S. coast. Generally,
I would be skeptical of Dr. Beter's charges,
especially his view that Vice President Rockefeller
is planning a seizure of the U.S. Government.

I will be in touch with you again.

With all good wishes,

Sincerely,

MILLICENT FENWICK
Member of Congress

THE JOINT CHIEFS OF STAFF
WASHINGTON, D.C. 20301

7 December 1976

Mr. William S. Bunte
8 Brian Drive
Bridgewater, New Jersey 08807

Dear Mr. Bunte

On behalf of President Ford, I am replying to your note
of November 28, 1976, regarding allegations by Dr. Peter
Beter that Soviet nuclear weapons have been placed in
US coastal waters.

General Brown has inquired into Dr. Beter's allegations
and found that they are not substantiated by the facts.
Additionally, General Brown has told Dr. Beter of this
country's capability to detect any such aggressive
actions by the Soviet Union or any other world power.

By way of background, I am enclosing a copy of a response
from the Director, Defense Intelligence Agency, to
Congressman P. A. Peyser on the same question. Also
included is a copy of General Brown's letter to Dr. Beter
on this subject.

Sincerely

W. Y. SMITH   Enclosures
Lt General, USAF
Assistant to the Chairman, JCS

Sometimes you do get answers.

For model rockets that David and
would fire in large open field.

...22% | Turnout.........................14% | Turnout........................33% | Turnout.......................24%

COURIER NEWS   4/13/2003

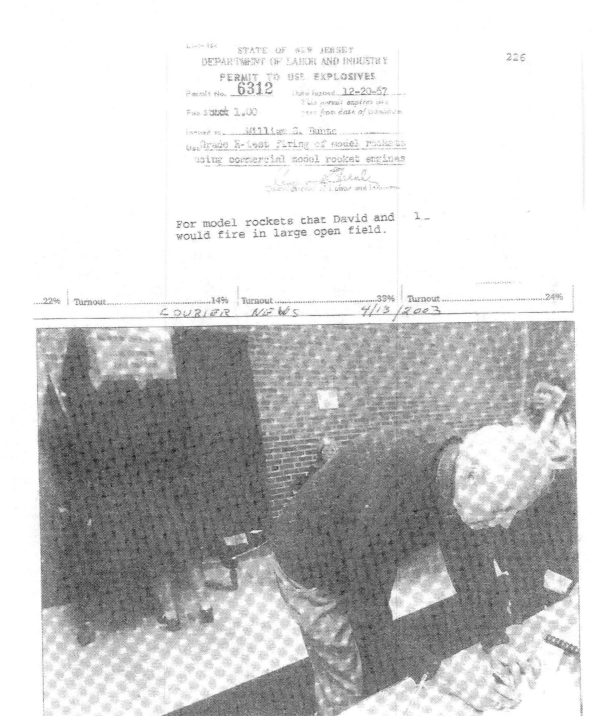

STAFF PHOTO BY WILLIAM D. BIRD

William Bunte of the Basking Ridge section of Bernards signs in before voting in the election for the Board of Education on Tuesday at Cedar Hill School in Bernards.

William Bunte of the Basking Ridge section of Bernards signs in before voting in the election for the Board of Education on Tuesday at Cedar Hill School in Bernards.

MISC.

Accidents and Traffic Violations.

About 40 years ago, I asked a friend, who was a New Jersey State Trooper, about speed limit enforcement. He said that if I were to keep within 5 mph of the speed limit, my chances of getting a ticket was very slight. I have followed his advice, and I haven't received a speeding ticket in the last 40 years. (On highways, most cars and trucks pass me, but that is O.K.)

I have been in a few accidents in the last 50 years, but none of them were my fault. I described one bad one in West Virginia earlier.

Another one was in Basking Ridge, NJ. There is a stop sign on on a local road at the bottom of a hill. I have been rear ended twice when I stopped there. The first time I wasn't injured. The driver said "I didn't think you were going to stop!". The second time a large SUV hit me hard after I had stopped. I had whiplash on my neck, and there was $5,500. damage to my car. The driver told the police officer, who came to the accident, that he had stopped, and then started up again. The officer said that was impossible with the amount of damage on my car.

As I was driving East on the Garden State Parkway towards NYC, I saw that the traffic had stopped. I stopped also and looked in the rear view mirrow. I saw a large car coming full speed at me. I could see that the driver's head was down so they couldn't see that the traffic had stopped. I took my foot off the brake and put my hand behind my head. My car was knocked ahead about 15 feet. (I had left about 20 feet between my car and the one in front of me). I didn't seem to be hurt, so I went to check on the person in the car that hit me. The driver, a women, was bleeding all over her head and face and she said she hurt all over. I called 911 and asked for an ambulance. Then I looked at her car. It was a large Mercedes. The entire front end was caved in and it was definitely not drivable. I looked at my Camry and saw only a few scratches on the rear bumper. I though that maybe the frame was damaged, so I took my car to the Camry dealer, and they could find no damage! I also had no whiplash, or any other injuries from the accident. I had never heard about "Taking your foot off the brake, and holding your head" when you are about to be hit by another car from the rear, so it must have been from the Holy Spirit or my Guardiang Angel!

I had a "an accident" that was my fault, and could have been very serious. I was driving South on Route 1 towards Trenton, NJ. I started to feel sleepy, so I started looking for an exit where I could get some coffee. The next thing I knew, I woke up and saw a four foot high cement barrier in front of me! (It was the divider between the North and South lanes, and the highway had curved to the right while I was asleep). I made a very sharp turn to the right (at 45 mph) and did not crash. I pulled over to the side of the highway and inspected the car. On the left side a small amout of the paint was scraped off. The engineer in me ran some calculations, and found that if I had turned 1/10,000 of a second later, I would have crashed! Before I left on this trip, I had prayed that God would watch over me as I drove, and He did - He knew exactly when to wake me up...

Chapter 12
Conclusion (Reflections)

It has been quite an experience writing this book. I can see how God has been guiding inspiring, and protecting me during my whole life. I see God's hand in almost all the decisions I have made during my 81 years. Just the one inspiration to take my fourth grade nun's suggestion to go to daily Mass, has improved my spiritual life dramatically. I am sure that the events that led me to be a part of Marriage Encounter, Charismatics and the People of Hope was from the Holy Spirit. Also my decision to put God first and family second (before work) in my priorities, was Gods doing. It has brought our family closer together. Even with my experience from working at so many various businesses, I can see God's hand in leading me to my consulting company (WSB Consultants) and Natural Energy, where I could work out of my home office.

I know that I didn't meet Lorna and Jean by chance. The Holy Spirit definitely had a hand in getting us together and He certainly knows how to pick them!

When I look back at all the times I could have died (from car accidents or near accidents, World War II, the typhoon at Okinawa, heart attack, and small intestine rupture) I am sure that God had a hand in saving me. Thank you Lord for all that you have done for me. I am truly grateful!

Printed in the United States
Bookmasters